MICHIGAN NONPROFIT CORPORATION ACT
2014 Edition

Updated through January 1, 2014

Michigan Legal Publishing Ltd.
QUICK DESK REFERENCE SERIES™

© 2014 Michigan Legal Publishing Ltd.

Academic and bulk discounts available at
www.michlp.com

THIS TEXT IS FOR EDUCATIONAL PURPOSES ONLY AND IS PROVIDED "AS IS" WITHOUT ANY WARRANTY, EXPRESS OR IMPLIED, INCLUDING, WITHOUT LIMITATION, ANY WARRANTY OF MERCHANTABILITY OR FITNESS FOR A PARTICULAR PURPOSE.

ISBN-13: 978-1495924651
ISBN-10: 1495924653

Contents

NONPROFIT CORPORATION ACT 1

Chapter 1 – General Provisions 1

450.2101 Short title. 1

450.2103 Construction and application of act. 1

450.2104 Definitions generally. 1

450.2105 Definitions; A, B. 2

450.2106 Definitions; C to E. 2

450.2107 Definitions; F to I. 3

450.2108 Definitions; M to P. 3

450.2109 Definitions; S. 4

450.2110 Definitions; T, V. 4

450.2121 Corporations to which act applicable; corporation organized under predecessor act. 4

450.2122 Statutory reference to repealed act as reference to this act; statutes not applicable to corporation. 5

450.2123 Applicability to corporation organized under other act not repealed by this act; organizations to which act inapplicable. 5

450.2124 Requirements of other acts not modified; compliance; inconsistency between acts. 6

450.2125 Applicability to commerce with foreign nations and among several states, and to corporations formed by act of congress. 6

450.2127 Effect of act on existing corporation, cause of action, liability, penalty, action, or special proceeding. 7

450.2129 Supplementation, alteration, amendment, or repeal of act by legislature. 7

450.2131 Submission of documents; delivery; endorsement; indexing; preparing and returning copy or original; public inspection; maintenance of records and files; effective date of document; fees. 7

450.2132 English language; numbers; articles of foreign corporation; signatures; contents of documents. 9

450.2133 Correction of document; certificate; effective date of corrected document. 10

450.2141 Taking action without notice and without lapse of prescribed period of time; waiver. 10

450.2142 Dispensing with notice or communication to person with whom communication unlawful; affidavit, certificate, or other instrument. 11

450.2143 Giving notice or communication by mail; electronic transmission as written notice. 11

450.2151 Refusal by administrator to file document promptly; notice of refusal to file; refusal or revocation of authorization of foreign corporation to conduct affairs in state; judicial review. 12

Chapter 2 – Formation 13

450.2201 Incorporators; signing and filing articles of incorporation. ... 13

450.2202 Articles of incorporation; contents. 13

450.2204 Articles of incorporation; provision pertaining to proposed compromise or arrangement or reorganization between corporation and creditors or shareholders. 14

450.2205 Articles of incorporation; including provision of MCL 450.2204; effect on creditors, shareholders, or members of corporation; administration and enforcement of provision by circuit court; restraining actions and proceedings against corporation; appointment and powers of temporary receiver. 15

450.2209 Articles of incorporation; additional provisions. 15

450.2212 Corporate name. 16

450.2213 Assuming name that implies corporation is banking corporation, insurance or surety company, or trust company prohibited. 18

450.2215 Reservation of right to use corporate name; application; duration; expiration; extension; transfer of right to exclusive use of reserved corporate name. 18

450.2217 Conduct of affairs under assumed name or names other than corporate name; assumption of same name by 2 or more corporations participating in partnership or joint venture; certificate of assumed name;

duration; extensions; notification of impending expiration; substantive rights to use of assumed name not created. 18

450.2221 Corporate existence to begin on effective date of articles; filing as conclusive evidence that conditions precedent fulfilled and corporation organized; exception. 19

450.2223 Selection of board and adoption of bylaws; first meeting; notice; quorum; transaction of business. 19

450.2231 Bylaws; adoption; amendment or repeal; contents. 20

450.2241 Registered office; resident agent. 20

450.2242 Change of registered office or resident agent; statement. 20

450.2243 Resident agent; resignation; notice; appointment of successor; termination of appointment of resigning agent. 21

450.2246 Resident agent; service of process, notice, or demand; resident agent as agent of director or officer in certain actions; forwarding process to director or officer 21

450.2251 Corporate purposes; conduct of lawful activities during war or national emergency. 22

450.2261 Corporate powers; inconsistency between certain acts; fixed limitation or term; waiver of right to perpetual existence; nonprofit power corporation. 22

450.2262 Existing incorporated association or society operating as corporation subject to act; payment of death or sick benefits; reserves; rules; investment of funds securing reserves; statement required of evidence of obligation to pay death and sick benefits. 25

450.2271 Act of corporation and transfer of property to or by corporation not invalid where corporation without capacity or power; assertion of lack of capacity or power. 26

450.2275 Agreement to pay rate of interest in excess of legal rate; defense of usury prohibited. 27

Chapter 3 – Structure **28**

450.2301 Payment or distribution of assets, income, or profit; conferring benefits on shareholders or members; compensation; distribution of assets upon dissolution; providing for payment of dividends or distribution of income or profit in articles or bylaws; application or distribution of profits; use, conveyance, or distribution of assets held by corporation for charitable purposes. 28

450.2302 Corporation organized upon nonstock basis. 29

450.2303 Corporation organized upon stock basis; provisions of articles and bylaws; issuance of shares; rights, preferences, and limitations of or upon shareholders; classes of shares; voting rights; transferability and cancellation of shares; rules of qualification and government. 29

450.2304 Corporation organized upon membership basis; provisions of articles or bylaws; rights, preferences, and limitations of or upon members; classes of members; voting rights; condominium association; homeowners or property owners association; transferability and termination of membership; rules of qualification and government; limitations on membership. 30

450.2305 Corporation organized upon directorship basis; members; voting; matters subject to action by board of directors. 31

450.2307 Subscription for shares or membership; enforceability; irrevocability; acceptance; consent to revocation; contract with corporation to purchase shares to be issued or treasury shares as subscription agreement. 32

450.2308 Subscription for shares or membership; payment; installments; call for payment ratable; retention of shares as security for performance by subscriber. 32

450.2309 Default in payment of amount due under subscription agreement; rights and duties of corporation; interpretation; limiting and adding to rights and remedies of corporation. 32

450.2310 Rescission of subscription under which part of shares issued and in which security interest retained as cancellation of shares. 34

450.2311 Fees or dues required as condition of shareholding or membership; fixing; enforcement. 34

450.2312 Issuance by corporation organized on stock basis of shares for fixed consideration; disposition of treasury shares. 34

450.2313 Corporation, unincorporated association, partnership, or other person as shareholder or member; officers and directors as director of corporation; rights, powers, privileges, and liabilities of shareholders or members. 34

450.2315 Consideration for issuance of shares; rights and privileges of subscribers when payment received by corporation; value of consideration; fully paid shares nonassessable. 35

450.2317 Obligation to pay unpaid portion of consideration for shares or membership as sole obligation; liability of person holding stock or membership in fiduciary or representative capacity; liability of assignee, transferee, or pledgee of shares, membership, or subscription for unpaid portion of consideration. 36

450.2327 Charges and expenses of organization or reorganization; sale or underwriting expenses and compensation; payment or allowance. . 36

450.2331 Representation of shares by certificates; signatures of officers and seal. 36

450.2332 Certificate representing shares; required statements. 37

450.2334 Lost or destroyed certificate; issuance of new certificate; bond. 37

450.2338 Issuing certificates for fractions of share; purposes; rights of holders; paying fair value of fractions of share in cash; issuing scrip in registered or bearer form exchangeable for full shares; conditions; providing opportunity to purchase additional fractions of share or scrip. 38

450.2361 Shares redeemable upon occurrence of specified event or events in cash, bonds, or other property; classes; sinking fund for redemption. 38

450.2363 Shares redeemable at option of shareholders in cash, bonds, or other property; classes; amendment to articles. 39

450.2365 Purchase or redemption by corporation of own shares under certain conditions prohibited. 39

450.2371 Cancellation of shares reacquired by corporation; retention of reacquired shares as treasury shares; status of cancelled shares. 40

450.2391 Conferring voting and inspection rights upon bond holders; signatures of officers. 40

Chapter 4 – Meetings 41

450.2401 Meetings of shareholders or members; location. 41

v

450.2402 Annual meeting of shareholders or members for election of directors and other business; failure to hold meeting at designated time or elect sufficient number of directors; adjournment of meeting; court order to hold meeting or election; quorum. 41

450.2403 Special meeting of shareholders or members; court order; quorum. 41

450.2404 Notice of time, place, and purposes of meeting of shareholders or members; manner; notice of adjourned meeting; notice not given; attendance at meeting as waiver of notice; participating and voting by remote communication. 42

450.2405 Shareholder or member participation in meeting by conference telephone or other means of remote communication; conditions; participation as presence in person at meeting; participating and voting by remote communication. 43

450.2406a Notice by electronic transmission. 44

450.2407 Taking corporate action without meeting; consent; notice; statement on filed certificate; consent by electronic transmission. 44

450.2411 Fixing record date for determination of shareholders or members entitled to notice and vote; effect of not fixing record date; applicability of determination to adjournment. 46

450.2413 Making and certifying list of shareholders or members entitled to vote at meeting or adjournment; requirements; noncompliance; adjournment of meeting; validity of action taken. 46

450.2415 Quorum; continuing to do business notwithstanding withdrawal of shareholders or members; adjournment of meeting; shareholders entitled to vote separately. 47

450.2421 Authorizing person to act for shareholder or member by proxy; signature; duration; revocability; methods of granting authority; use of facsimile or reproduction. 48

450.2422 Irrevocable proxy. 49

450.2423 Revocability of proxy. 49

450.2431 Inspectors at shareholders' or members' meeting; waiver; appointment and duties; failure to appoint; vacancy; report; evidence. 50

450.2441 Voting generally. 51

450.2442 Voting as class. 51

450.2443 Grouping of members in local units; basis; purpose; actions authorized by bylaws; incorporation and powers of local units; powers, rights, and privileges of elected representatives or delegates. 52

450.2444 Voting by corporation or business corporation; voting of pledged shares. 53

450.2445 Voting of shares or membership held by person in representative or fiduciary capacity or held jointly by fiduciaries. 53

450.2446 Voting of shares or membership held by joint tenants or tenants in common. 54

450.2447 Treasury shares; shares of corporation held by another corporation or business corporation; voting. 54

450.2448 Redemption of shares; voting. 54

450.2451 Voting for directors 55

450.2455 Action requiring vote or concurrence of greater proportion of shares, members, or class than required by act; amendment of articles. 55

450.2461 Agreement as to voting rights. 55

450.2471 Shares as personal property; transfer; applicability of MCL 440.8101 to 440.8601. 56

450.2481 Issuing or delivering unissued or treasury shares; preemptive rights. 56

450.2485 Books, records, and minutes. 56

450.2487 Mailing balance sheet and statements to shareholder or member upon request; examination of minutes and records; compelling production of books, records, and minutes; extracts. 57

450.2491 Action by shareholder or member in right of corporation to procure judgment; allegations. 57

450.2492 Discontinuance, compromise, or settlement of action authorized by MCL 450.2491; approval; notice; expense; award and recovery. 58

450.2493 Action brought in right of corporation; awarding plaintiff or claimant reasonable expenses; accounting; applicability of section;

requiring plaintiff to pay expenses where action brought without reasonable cause. 58

Chapter 5 – Management 60

450.2501 Management of business and affairs of corporation by board; qualifications of directors; powers of board. 60

450.2501a Board of directors; minimum age; requirements. 60

450.2505 Board; number, term, and election or appointment of directors; resignation of director; number of directors on effective date of amendatory act. 60

450.2506 Dividing directors into 2 or more classes; election or appointment; term; expiration; election of directors by shareholders or members of class. 61

450.2511 Removal of director or entire board. 62

450.2515 Filling of vacancies; increase in number of directors; special meeting where no directors in office. 63

450.2521 Regular or special meetings of board; location; notice; waiver; participation by means of conference telephone or other remote communication. 63

450.2523 Quorum; vote constituting action of board or committee; amendment of bylaws. 64

450.2525 Taking action without meeting; consent. 64

450.2527 Designation of committees; membership; alternates; term; providing for election or appointment of committees in articles or bylaws. 64

450.2528 Committee designated pursuant to MCL 450.2527; powers and authority. 65

450.2531 Officers of corporation; election or appointment; person holding 2 or more offices; term of office; authority and duties. 66

450.2535 Removal of officer; suspension of authority to act; contract rights; resignation of officer; notice. 66

450.2541 Director or officer; discharge of duties; compliance; liability of volunteer director; action against director or officer for failure to perform duties. 67

450.2545 Transaction between corporation and directors or officers, or between corporation and corporation or business corporation, firm, or association in which directors or officers interested, not void or voidable; conditions. 68

450.2546 Burden of establishing validity of contract described in MCL 450.2545; grounds; counting common or interested directors in determining presence of quorum; compensation of directors; approval of shareholders or members. 68

450.2548 Loan, guaranty, or assistance by corporation for officer or employee; corporation as charitable purpose corporation. 69

450.2551 Liability of directors for certain corporate actions; liability of shareholder or member accepting or receiving unauthorized distribution. 69

450.2552 Rights of director against whom claim successfully asserted under MCL 450.2551. 70

450.2553 Presence or absence of director at meeting at which action referred to in MCL 450.2551 taken; presumption; dissent. 71

450.2554 Commencement of action under MCL 450.2551 or 450.2552. 71

450.2556 Volunteer's acts or omissions; claim for monetary damages. 72

450.2561 Indemnification of director, officer, partner, trustee, employee, nondirector volunteer, or agent in connection with action, suit, or proceeding; conditions; presumption. 72

450.2562 Indemnification against expenses of director, officer, partner, trustee, employee, nondirector volunteer, or agent in connection with action or suit by or in right of corporation; conditions; limitations. 73

450.2563 Indemnification against expenses of director, officer, employee, nondirector volunteer, or agent successful in defense of action, suit, or proceeding referred to in MCL 450.2561 or 450.2562; authorization; determination; indemnification for portion of expenses. 73

450.2564 Advance payment by corporation of expenses incurred in defending action, suit, or proceeding described in MCL 450.2561 or 450.2562; repayment. 74

ix

450.2565 Indemnification or advancement of expenses not exclusive of other rights; limitation; continuation of indemnification. 75

450.2567 Purchase and maintenance of insurance on behalf of director, officer, employee, nondirector volunteer, or agent. 75

450.2569 Scope of "corporation" for purposes of MCL 450.2561 to 450.2567; effect. 76

Chapter 6 – Amending Corporate Documents 77

450.2601 Amendment of articles of incorporation; contents. 77

450.2602 Amendment of articles of incorporation; purposes. 77

450.2611 Amendment of articles by incorporators; manner of adoption; notice of meeting; vote on proposed amendment; requirements; adoption; number of amendments acted upon at 1 meeting; certificate of amendment. 78

450.2615 Voting as class upon proposed amendment 79

450.2631 Certificate of amendment; signing or execution; filing; contents. 80

450.2641 Integrating provisions of articles into single instrument; adoption of restated articles of incorporation; amendments subject to other provisions of act. 80

450.2642 Restated articles of incorporation; designation; required statements; omitted provisions. 80

450.2643 Restated articles of incorporation; execution; filing; effect. 81

450.2651 Abandonment of amendment; certificate. 81

Chapter 7 – Merger and Consolidation 82

450.2701 Merger or consolidation of domestic corporations; plan; contents. 82

450.2703 Plan of merger or consolidation; approval or authorization; voting; notice of meeting. 83

450.2707 Certificate of merger or certificate of consolidation; execution and filing; contents; effective date. 83

450.2721 Effect of merger or consolidation. 84

450.2722 Surviving or new corporation; rights, privileges, immunities, and franchises; liabilities and obligations; prosecution of existing claim or pending action or proceeding; rights of creditors; lien upon property of corporation. 84

450.2723 Changes in articles stated in plan of merger; effect; statements in plan of consolidation as original articles of new corporation. 85

450.2732 Effect of merger or consolidation authorized by MCL 450.2731. 86

450.2736 Merger or consolidation of domestic corporations and domestic or foreign business corporations; procedure; compliance with applicable laws; plan of merger or consolidation; applicability of act to surviving or new corporation or business corporation governed by laws of other jurisdiction; liability of corporation or business corporation; service of process.................. 86

450.2737 Effect of merger or consolidation where surviving or new corporation is domestic corporation, domestic business corporation, or foreign business corporation. 87

450.2741 Abandonment of merger or consolidation; certificate of abandonment.................. 88

450.2753 Disposition of property and assets of corporation; approval; notice of meeting; statement; authorization; fixing terms or conditions and consideration; voting; abandonment. 88

Chapter 8 – Dissolution 90

450.2801 Dissolution of corporation; methods; summary dissolution of corporation whose assets disposed of under court order in receivership or bankruptcy proceedings; filing copy of order with administrator. .. 90

450.2803 Dissolution of corporation by action of incorporators or directors; conditions; certificate of dissolution. 90

450.2804 Dissolution of corporation by action of shareholders, members, or board; resolution; approval or authorization; notice; voting; certificate. 91

450.2805 Provision in articles permitting shareholders, members, or directors to require dissolution authorized; plan of distribution of assets; execution and filing of certificate of dissolution; noting existence of provision on face of share certificates or membership certificates. 92

450.2811 Revocation of dissolution proceedings; resolution of board; approval; notice of meeting; voting; certificate of revocation. 93

450.2815 Renewal of corporate existence. 94

450.2817 Effect of filing certificate of revocation of dissolution or renewal of corporate existence; accrued penalty or liability; adoption of different name. 95

450.2821 Action by attorney general for dissolution of corporation; grounds. 95

450.2823 Dissolution of corporation by judgment in action brought by director, shareholder, or member; proof. 96

450.2825 Adjudging dissolution and liquidation of assets and affairs of corporation by circuit court in action filed by shareholder, member, or director; grounds; making order or granting relief other than dissolution. 96

450.2833 Dissolved corporation; continuation of corporate existence; conduct of affairs. 97

450.2834 Dissolved corporation and officers, directors, shareholders, and members; manner of functioning. 98

450.2841 Notice to creditors; "creditor" defined. 98

450.2842 Mailing notice to creditor of corporation; failure to file claim as bar to enforcement; applicability. 99

450.2843 Rejection of claim filed by creditor; notice; failure to commence action as bar to enforcement of claim. 99

450.2851 Application for judgment that affairs of corporation and liquidation of assets continue under supervision of court; orders and judgments; permitting creditor to file claim or commence action. 100

450.2855 Application and distribution of assets upon dissolution. 100

450.2861 Plan of reorganization; action by directors, shareholders, or members not required to put plan into effect. 101

450.2862 Powers of corporation under reorganization; issuing shares of capital stock and bonds for consideration specified in plan of reorganization. 102

450.2863 Document filed or recorded to accomplish corporate purpose pursuant to plan of reorganization; making, execution, and acknowledgment; contents; filing. 102

450.2864 Reversal or vacation of reorganization plan; filing of other or further certificates or documents; effect; fees. 103

Chapter 9 – Renewal and Reporting 104

450.2901 Report of corporation; contents; electronic transmission; distribution to shareholder, member, or director. 104

450.2911 Annual report to administrator; filing; contents. 104

450.2913 Destruction or disposition of certain records. 105

450.2922 Failure of domestic or foreign corporation to file annual report or pay filing fee; automatic dissolution or revocation of certificate of authority; dissolution of charitable purpose corporation; notice; right to certificate of good standing. 105

450.2923 Extension of time for filing report; reporting failure or neglect under MCL 450.2922, 450.2931, and 450.2932 to attorney general; action by attorney general; certificate of mailing as evidence. 106

450.2924 Annual reports due or deficient prior to date of act; penalties. 106

450.2925 Renewal of corporate existence or certificate of authority following dissolution or revocation. 106

450.2931 Wilful false statement in report; additional penalty. 107

450.2932 Prohibited conduct as misdemeanor; fine. 107

450.2935 Authorizing, signing, or making false statement or notice; authorizing or making wrongful alteration of book, record, or account; liability; commencement of action. 108

Chapter 10 – Foreign Corporations and Misc. Provisions 109

450.3001 Foreign corporation authorized to conduct affairs in this state on effective date of act; rights and privileges; duties, restrictions, penalties, and liabilities. 109

450.3002 Foreign corporation receiving certificate of authority under act; rights and privileges; duties, restrictions, penalties, and liabilities. 109

450.3003 Foreign corporation conducting affairs without certificate of authority; duties, restrictions, penalties, and liabilities. 109

450.3011 Foreign corporation; certificate of authority required; extent of authorization to conduct affairs in state. 110

450.3012 Foreign corporation not considered to be conducting affairs in state; activities; applicability of section. 110

450.3015 Application of foreign corporation for certificate of authority to conduct affairs in state; contents. 111

450.3016 Application of foreign corporation for certificate of authority to conduct affairs in state; attachments; fees; issuance of certificate; duration of authority...........111

450.3021 Foreign corporation authorized to conduct affairs in state; filing with administrator copy of amendment of articles or certificate of merger, consolidation, or similar corporate action...........112

450.3031 Foreign corporation authorized to conduct affairs in state; withdrawal; certificate; application...........112

450.3032 Issuance of certificate of withdrawal; conditions; effect....113

450.3035 Foreign corporation authorized to conduct affairs in state; termination or cancellation of authority or existence; filing information, certificate, order, or judgment with administrator; payment of fees; certificate of withdrawal. 113

450.3041 Revocation of certificate of authority of foreign corporation to conduct affairs in state; grounds. 114

450.3042 Revocation of certificate of authority of foreign corporation to conduct affairs in state; notice of default under MCL 450.3031; certificate of revocation. 114

450.3051 Action commenced by foreign corporation without certificate of authority prohibited; applicability of prohibition; effect of failure to obtain certificate of authority on validity of contract and act of corporation; defense of action or proceeding...........115

450.3055 Foreign corporation conducting affairs in state without certificate of authority; penalty. 115

450.3060 Fees; payment; certification of file or record; refund; waiver. 116

450.3061 Fee for privilege of exercising franchises in state. 117

450.3098 Repeal of acts and parts of acts. 118

450.3099 Effective date of act. 118

Chapter 11 – Cooperatives 119

450.3100 Short title. 119

450.3101 Applicability of act and chapter; amendment of articles or bylaws; exemption. 119

450.3102 Controlling definitions. 120

450.3103 Definitions; C to F. 120

450.3104 Definitions; M to U. 121

450.3107 Inconsistent provisions inapplicable to chapter. 122

450.3109 Requirements of MCL 460.1 et seq. not modified; effect of economic activity conducted by cooperative. 122

450.3121 Articles of incorporation; requirement. 122

450.3123 Use of term "cooperative," "co-op," "consumer cooperative," or any variation thereof. 122

450.3125 Adoption of initial bylaws; ratification or amendment; contents of bylaws. 123

450.3131 Organization on nonstock membership basis. 124

450.3132 Membership; notice of qualifications. 124

450.3133 Classification. 124

450.3134 Cooperative organized on member capital basis, member fee basis, or basis combining member capital and membership fee; powers. 124

450.3135 Net savings; determination, allocation, distribution, and use; apportionment of losses. 125

450.3136 Certificate; issuance; contents; restrictions on dividends. . 126

450.3137 Nonvoting investment certificate or bond. 127

450.3138 Advising persons in writing; statement on membership certificate. 127

450.3139 Redemption of member capital; failure to patronize cooperative; notice of redemption; failure to respond and claim payment; failure to claim refunds of patronage capital, deposits, and fees; failure of nonmember patron to pay in or accumulate full member capital or comply with bylaws. 128

450.3141 Meetings; petitions; signatures; quorum. 129

xv

450.3143 Alternative notice of regular meeting....................................129

450.3144 Proxies; voting by mail ballot, referendum, or electronic transmission. 129

450.3145 Amendments; affirmative vote of majority. 130

450.3146 Effective date of adopted action; confirmation vote; filing with administrator. 130

450.3147 Dispute resolution body. 131

450.3148 Purchase or sale under execution, in course of bankruptcy, or by legal process or operation of law; pledge of certificate; assignment of proprietary lease or other agreement. 131

450.3149 Books for recording operations; annual report, balance sheet, and income statement; certified report of condition; copies of reports; mailings at request and expense of member; notice of member's desire to be contacted by other members regarding proposal. 131

450.3151 Initial board of directors; membership; term. 132

450.3152 Board of directors; election or appointment other than by vote of membership. 133

450.3153 Affiliation with another organization; section inapplicable to allocations of net savings. 133

450.3161 Amendment to articles of incorporation; calling special meeting; consideration of proposed amendment. 133

450.3162 Distribution of assets generally. 133

450.3183 Distribution of assets upon dissolution; distribution of assets held for charitable or similar purpose; redemption of investment certificates. 134

450.3191 Foreign cooperative. 134

450.3192 Election by corporation to accept act and chapter; procedure; effect of filing certificate of election. 135

NONPROFIT CORPORATION ACT

Act 162 of 1982 (as amended)

AN ACT to revise, consolidate, and classify the laws relating to the organization and regulation of certain nonprofit corporations; to prescribe their duties, rights, powers, immunities, and liabilities; to provide for the authorization of foreign nonprofit corporations within this state; to impose certain duties on certain state departments; to prescribe fees; to prescribe penalties for violations of this act; and to repeal certain acts and parts of acts.

The People of the State of Michigan enact:

Chapter 1 – General Provisions

450.2101 Short title.

Sec. 101.

This act shall be known and may be cited as the "nonprofit corporation act".

450.2103 Construction and application of act.

Sec. 103.

This act shall be liberally construed and applied to promote its underlying purposes and policies which include:
(a) To simplify, clarify, and modernize the law governing nonprofit corporations.
(b) To provide a general corporate form for the conduct of lawful nonprofit activities with such variations and modifications from the form as interested parties in any corporation may agree upon, subject only to overriding interests of this state and of third parties.

450.2104 Definitions generally.

Sec. 104.

The definitions contained in sections 105 to 110 shall control only in the interpretation of this act, unless the context otherwise requires.

450.2105 Definitions; A, B.

Sec. 105.

(1) "Administrator" means the director of commerce or the head of any other agency or department authorized by law to administer this act, or a designated representative of that person.
(2) "Articles of incorporation" includes (a) the original articles of incorporation or any other instrument filed or issued under any statute to organize a domestic or foreign corporation, as amended, supplemented, or restated by certificates of amendment, merger, or consolidation, or other certificates or instruments filed or issued under any statute; or (b) a special act or charter creating a domestic or foreign corporation, as amended, supplemented, or restated.
(3) "Assets" means the properties and rights entered upon the books of a corporation in accordance with generally accepted accounting principles, or the current fair market value of such properties and rights.
(4) "Authorized shares" means shares of all classes that a corporation is authorized to issue.
(5) "Board" means the board of directors or trustees or other governing board of a corporation.
(6) "Bonds" includes secured and unsecured bonds, debentures and notes.
(7) "Business corporation" or "domestic business corporation" means a corporation for profit organized under Act No. 284 of the Public Acts of 1972, as amended, being sections 450.1101 to 450.2099 of the Michigan Compiled Laws, or existing on January 1, 1973 and theretofore formed under any other statute of this state for a purpose for which a corporation for profit may be organized under that act.

450.2106 Definitions; C to E.

Sec. 106.

(1) "Charitable purpose corporation" means a nonprofit corporation that meets any of the following:
   (a) Is exempt or qualifies for exemption under section 501(c)(3) of the internal revenue code, 26 USC 501.

(b) Is a corporation whose purposes, structure, or activities are exclusively those that are described in section 501(c)(3) of the internal revenue code, 26 USC 501.
(c) Is a corporation organized or held out to be organized exclusively for 1 or more charitable purposes.

(2) "Corporation" or "domestic corporation" means a nonprofit corporation.
(3) "Director" means an individual who is a member of the board of a corporation. The term is synonymous with "trustee" of a corporation or other similar designation.
(4) "Electronic transmission" or "electronically transmitted" means any form of communication that meets all of the following:
  (a) It does not directly involve the physical transmission of paper.
  (b) It creates a record that may be retained and retrieved by the recipient.
  (c) It may be directly reproduced in paper form by the recipient through an automated process.

450.2107 Definitions; F to I.

Sec. 107.

(1) "Foreign business corporation" means a corporation for profit organized under laws other than the laws of this state, which includes in its purposes a purpose for which a corporation may be organized under Act No. 284 of the Public Acts of 1972, as amended.
(2) "Foreign corporation" means a corporation organized under laws other than the laws of this state conducting affairs in this state for a purpose or purposes for which a corporation may be organized under this act.
(3) "Insolvent" means being unable to pay debts as they become due in the usual course of a debtor's business.

450.2108 Definitions; M to P.

Sec. 108.

(1) "Member" means a person having a membership in a corporation in accordance with the provisions of its articles of incorporation or bylaws.
(2) "Nondirector volunteer" means an individual, other than a volunteer director, performing services for a nonprofit corporation who does not

receive compensation or any other type of consideration for the services other than reimbursement for expenses actually incurred.
(3) "Nonprofit corporation" means a corporation incorporated to carry out any lawful purpose or purposes not involving pecuniary profit or gain for its directors, officers, shareholders, or members.
(4) "Person" means an individual, partnership, corporation, association, or any other legal entity.
(5) "Predecessor act" means an act or part of an act repealed by this act, or an act or part of an act repealed by an act that this act repeals.

450.2109 Definitions; S.

Sec. 109.

"Shares" means the units into which interests of shareholders in a corporation are divided.

450.2110 Definitions; T, V.

Sec. 110.

(1) "Treasury shares" means shares which have been issued, have been subsequently acquired by a corporation, and have not been canceled. Treasury shares are issued shares, but not outstanding shares.
(2) "Volunteer director" means a director who does not receive anything of more than nominal value from the corporation for serving as a director other than reasonable per diem compensation and reimbursement for actual, reasonable, and necessary expenses incurred by a director in his or her capacity as a director.

450.2121 Corporations to which act applicable; corporation organized under predecessor act.

Sec. 121.

(1) Except as otherwise provided in this act or by other law, this act applies to all of the following:
   (a) Every domestic corporation organized under this act or under a predecessor act, for a purpose or purposes for which a corporation might be organized under this act.

(b) Every foreign corporation which is authorized to conduct affairs in this state.
(c) Any other domestic corporation or foreign corporation to the extent provided under this act or any law governing such corporation.

(2) A corporation organized under a predecessor act is subject to this act except to the extent that this act conflicts with the articles and bylaws of the corporation lawfully made pursuant to the predecessor act. The corporation may amend its articles and bylaws to bring itself in conformity with this act.

450.2122 Statutory reference to repealed act as reference to this act; statutes not applicable to corporation.

Sec. 122.

(1) A reference in any statute of this state to parts of any act which are repealed by this act is deemed to be a reference to this act, unless the context requires otherwise.
(2) The following statutes do not apply to a corporation, as defined in section 106:
  (a) Chapter 55 of the Revised Statutes of 1846, entitled "general provisions relating to corporations", as amended, being sections 450.504 to 450 525 of the Michigan Compiled Laws.
  (b) Act No. 156 of the Public Acts of 1955, being sections 450.701 to 450.704 of the Michigan Compiled Laws.

450.2123 Applicability to corporation organized under other act not repealed by this act; organizations to which act inapplicable.

Sec. 123.

(1) Unless otherwise provided in, and to the extent not inconsistent with, the act under which a corporation is or has been formed, this act applies to a corporation that is or has been organized under an act other than this act and not repealed by this act.
(2) A corporation covered by subsection (1) includes, but is not limited to, all of the following:
  (a) A cooperative corporation classified as a nonprofit corporation under section 98 of 1931 PA 327, MCL 450.98.
  (b) A secret society or lodge.

(c) A trustee corporation holding property for charitable, religious, benevolent, educational, or other public benefit purposes.
(d) A church trustee corporation.
(e) An educational corporation that is organized as a trustee corporation or a nonprofit corporation.
(f) An ecclesiastical corporation.
(g) A public building corporation.
(h) A street railway under the nonprofit street railway act, 1867 PA 35, MCL 472.1 to 472.31.
(3) Except as provided in subsection (2)(h), this act does not apply to insurance, surety, credit unions, savings and loan associations, fraternal benefit societies, railroad, bridge, or tunnel companies, union depot companies, and banking corporations.

450.2124 Requirements of other acts not modified; compliance; inconsistency between acts.

Sec. 124.

(1) This act does not modify the requirements of the following:
   (a) The supervision of trustees for charitable purposes act, 1961 PA 101, MCL 14.251 to 14.266.
   (b) 1965 PA 169, MCL 450.251 to 450.253.
   (c) The charitable organizations and solicitations act, 1975 PA 169, MCL 400.271 to 400.294.
   (d) The uniform prudent management of institutional funds act.
   (e) The career development and distance learning act, 2002 PA 36, MCL 390.1571 to 390.1579.
(2) A corporation subject to 1 or more of the acts listed in subsection (1) shall comply with those acts and shall comply with this act. If there is any inconsistency between those acts and this act, those acts shall control.

450.2125 Applicability to commerce with foreign nations and among several states, and to corporations formed by act of congress.

Sec. 125.

This act applies to commerce with foreign nations and among the several states and to corporations formed by or under any act of congress, only to the extent permitted under the constitution and laws of the United States.

450.2127 Effect of act on existing corporation, cause of action, liability, penalty, action, or special proceeding.

Sec. 127.

(1) Except as provided in section 261(3), this act does not affect the duration of a corporation which exists on the effective date of this act. An existing corporation and its shareholders, members, directors, and officers have the same rights and are subject to the same limitations, restrictions, liabilities, and penalties as a corporation formed under this act, and its shareholders, members, directors, and officers.

(2) This act does not affect a cause of action, liability, penalty, or action or special proceeding, which on the effective date of this act is accrued, existing, incurred, or pending, but the same may be asserted, enforced, prosecuted, or defended as if this act had not been enacted.

450.2129 Supplementation, alteration, amendment, or repeal of act by legislature.

Sec. 129.

This act may be supplemented, altered, amended, or repealed by the legislature and every corporation, domestic or foreign, to which this act applies is bound thereby.

450.2131 Submission of documents; delivery; endorsement; indexing; preparing and returning copy or original; public inspection; maintenance of records and files; effective date of document; fees.

Sec. 131.

(1) A document required or permitted to be filed under this act shall be submitted by delivering the document to the administrator together with the fees and accompanying documents required by law. The administrator may establish a procedure for accepting delivery of a document submitted under this subsection by facsimile or other

electronic transmission. However, by December 31, 2006, the administrator shall establish a procedure for accepting delivery of a document submitted under this subsection by electronic mail or over the internet. Beginning January 1, 2007, the administrator shall accept delivery of documents submitted by electronic mail or over the internet.

(2) If a document submitted under subsection (1) substantially conforms to the requirements of this act, the administrator shall endorse upon it the word "filed" with the administrator's official title and the dates of receipt and of filing, and shall file and index the document or a reproduction of the document pursuant to the records reproduction act, 1992 PA 116, MCL 24.401 to 24.406, in the administrator's office. If requested at the time of the delivery of the document to the administrator's office, the administrator shall include the hour of filing in the endorsement on the document.

(3) The administrator shall return a copy of a document filed under subsection (2), other than an annual report, or, at his or her discretion, the original, to the person who submitted the document for filing. The administrator shall mark the filing date on the copy or original before returning it or, if the document was submitted by electronic mail or over the internet, may provide proof of the filing date to the person who submitted the document for filing in another manner determined by the administrator.

(4) The records and files of the administrator relating to corporations shall be open to reasonable inspection by the public. The administrator may maintain the records or files either in their original form or in the form of reproductions pursuant to the records reproduction act, 1992 PA 116, MCL 24.401 to 24.406.

(5) The administrator may make copies of any documents filed under this act, or any predecessor act, pursuant to the records reproduction act, 1992 PA 116, MCL 24.401 to 24.406, and may destroy the originals of the reproduced documents.

(6) A document filed under subsection (2) is effective at the time it is endorsed unless a subsequent effective time, not later than 90 days after the date of delivery, is set forth in the document.

(7) The administrator shall charge 1 of the following nonrefundable fees if expedited filing of a document by the administrator is requested and the administrator shall retain the revenue collected under this subsection and the department shall use it to carry out its duties required by law:
    (a) For any filing that a person requests the administrator to complete within 1 hour on the same day as the day of the request, $1,000.00.

The department may establish a deadline by which a person must submit a request for filing under this subdivision.

(b) For any filing that a person requests the administrator to complete within 2 hours on the same day as the day of the request, $500.00. The department may establish a deadline by which a person must submit a request for filing under this subdivision.

(c) Except for a filing request under subdivision (a) or (b), for the filing of any formation or qualification document that a person requests the administrator to complete on the same day as the day of the request, $100.00. The department may establish a deadline by which a person must submit a request for filing under this subdivision.

(d) Except for a filing request under subdivision (a) or (b), for the filing of any other document concerning an existing domestic corporation or a qualified foreign corporation that a person requests the administrator to complete on the same day as the day of the request, $200.00. The department may establish a deadline by which a person must submit a request for filing under this subdivision.

(e) For the filing of any formation or qualification document that a person requests the administrator to complete within 24 hours of the time the administrator receives the request, $50.00.

(f) For the filing of any other document concerning an existing domestic corporation or a qualified foreign corporation that a person requests the administrator to complete within 24 hours of the time the administrator receives the request, $100.00.

450.2132 English language; numbers; articles of foreign corporation; signatures; contents of documents.

Sec. 132.

(1) A document filed with the administrator shall be in the English language, except that the corporate name need not be in the English language if written in English letters or Arabic or Roman numerals, and the articles of incorporation of a foreign corporation need not be in the English language.

(2) A document required or permitted to be filed under this act which is also required by this act to be executed on behalf of the corporation, shall be signed in ink by the chairperson or vice-chairperson of the board or the president or a vice-president. If the corporation is in the hands of a

receiver, trustee, or other court appointed officer, the document shall be signed in ink by the fiduciary or the majority of them, if there are more than 1. The name of a person signing the document and the capacity in which the person signs, shall be stated beneath or opposite the signature. The document may, but need not, contain:

(a) The corporate seal.
(b) An attestation by the secretary or an assistant secretary of the corporation.
(c) An acknowledgment or proof.

450.2133 Correction of document; certificate; effective date of corrected document.

Sec. 133.

If a document relating to a domestic or foreign corporation filed with the administrator under this act is an inaccurate record of the corporation action referred to in the document or was defectively or erroneously executed, or the document was electronically transmitted and the electronic transmission was defective, the document may be corrected by filing with the administrator a certificate of correction on behalf of the corporation. A certificate entitled "certificate of correction of... (correct title of document and name of corporation)" shall be signed as provided in this act with respect to the document being corrected and filed with the administrator. The certificate shall set forth the name of the corporation, the date the document to be corrected was filed by the administrator, the provision in the document as corrected or eliminated, and if the execution was defective, the proper execution. The corrected document is effective in its corrected form as of its original filing date except as to a person who relied upon the inaccurate portion of the document and was, as a result of the inaccurate portion of the document, adversely affected by the correction.

450.2141 Taking action without notice and without lapse of prescribed period of time; waiver.

Sec. 141.

When, under this act or the articles of incorporation or bylaws of a corporation or by the terms of an agreement or instrument, a corporation or the board or any committee of the board may take action after notice to any person or after lapse of a prescribed period of time, the action may be taken without notice and without lapse of the period of time, if at any time before or after the action is completed the person entitled to notice or to participate in the action to be taken or, in case of a shareholder or member, by the shareholder or member's attorney-in-fact, submits a signed waiver or a waiver by electronic transmission of the requirements.

450.2142 Dispensing with notice or communication to person with whom communication unlawful; affidavit, certificate, or other instrument.

Sec. 142.

When a notice or communication is required to be given to a person by this act, by the articles of incorporation or bylaws, or by the terms of an agreement or instrument relating to the internal affairs of the corporation, or as a condition precedent to taking corporate action, and communication with the person is then unlawful under a statute of this state or the United States or a rule, regulation, proclamation, or order issued under any of those statutes, the giving of the notice or communication to the person is not required and there is no duty to apply for a license or other permission to do so. An affidavit, certificate or other instrument which is required to be made or filed as proof of the giving of a notice or communication required by this act, if the notice or communication to any person is dispensed with under this section, shall include a statement that the notice or communication was not given to any person with whom communication is unlawful. The affidavit, certificate or other instrument is as effective for all purposes as though the notice or communication had been personally given to the person.

450.2143 Giving notice or communication by mail; electronic transmission as written notice.

Sec. 143.

(1) When a notice or communication is required or permitted by this act to be given by mail, it shall be mailed, except as otherwise provided in this act, to the person to whom it is directed at the address designated by that person for that purpose or, if none is designated, at that person's last known address. The notice or communication is given when deposited, with postage prepaid, in a post office or official depository under the exclusive care and custody of the United States postal service. The

mailing shall be registered, certified, or other first class mail except where otherwise provided in this act.
(2) When a notice is required or permitted by this act to be given in writing, electronic transmission is written notice.
(3) When a notice or communication is permitted by this act to be transmitted electronically, the notice or communication is given when electronically transmitted to the person entitled to the notice or communication in a manner authorized by the person.

450.2151 Refusal by administrator to file document promptly; notice of refusal to file; refusal or revocation of authorization of foreign corporation to conduct affairs in state; judicial review.

Sec. 151.

(1) If the administrator refuses to promptly file a document, other than an annual report, submitted for filing under this act, the administrator shall within 10 days after receipt from the person submitting the document for filing of a written request for the filing of the document give written notice of the refusal to file the document to that person, specifying the reasons for the refusal to file the document. If the document was not originally submitted by electronic transmission, the administrator shall not give the written notice by electronic transmission. The person may seek judicial review of the refusal to file the document pursuant to sections 103, 104, and 106 of the administrative procedures act of 1969, 1969 PA 306, MCL 24.303, 24.304, and 24.306.
(2) If the administrator refuses or revokes the authorization of a foreign corporation to conduct affairs in this state pursuant to this act, the foreign corporation may seek judicial review pursuant to sections 103, 104, and 106 of the administrative procedures act of 1969, 1969 PA 306, MCL 24.303, 24.304, and 24.306.

Chapter 2 – Formation

450.2201 Incorporators; signing and filing articles of incorporation.

Sec. 201.

(1) One or more persons may be the incorporators of a corporation by signing in ink and filing articles of incorporation for the corporation.
(2) If there are 3 or more incorporators of a corporation, the incorporators may, by suitable resolution adopted by the incorporators at the organization meeting or by written instrument, designate any 1 among themselves to sign the articles of incorporation for that person and the remainder of the incorporators, in which case a copy of the resolution duly certified by the person who acted as secretary at the organization meeting shall be made a part of and filed with the articles of incorporation.

450.2202 Articles of incorporation; contents.

Sec. 202.

The articles of incorporation shall contain:
(a) The name of the corporation.
(b) The purposes for which the corporation is organized. It shall not be sufficient to state substantially that the corporation may engage in any activity within the purposes for which a corporation may be organized under this act. A corporation which proposes to conduct educational purposes shall state such purposes and shall comply with all requirements of sections 170 to 177 of Act No. 327 of the Public Acts of 1931, as amended, being sections 450.170 to 450.177 of the Michigan Compiled Laws.
(c) In the case of a corporation organized on a stock basis, the aggregate number of shares which the corporation has authority to issue.
(d) In the case of a corporation organized on a stock basis, if the shares are, or are to be, divided into classes, to the extent that the designations, numbers, relative rights, preferences, and limitations have been determined: the designation of each class; the number of shares in each class; and a statement of the relative rights, preferences, and limitations of the shares of each class.

(e) In the case of a corporation organized on a nonstock basis, a description and statement of the value of any assets of the corporation classified as to real and personal property and the terms of the general scheme of financing the corporation.
(f) In the case of a corporation organized on a nonstock basis, a statement that the corporation is organized on a membership basis or a statement that the corporation is organized on a directorship basis.
(g) The street address, and the mailing address if different from the street address, of the corporation's initial registered office and the name of the corporation's initial resident agent at that address.
(h) The names and addresses of all the incorporators, whether or not fewer than all the incorporators sign the articles pursuant to section 201(2).
(i) The duration of the corporation if other than perpetual.

450.2204 Articles of incorporation; provision pertaining to proposed compromise or arrangement or reorganization between corporation and creditors or shareholders.

Sec. 204.

The articles of incorporation may contain the following provision or the substance thereof: When a compromise or arrangement or a plan of reorganization of this corporation is proposed between this corporation and its creditors or any class of them or between this corporation and its shareholders, members, or any class of them, a court of equity jurisdiction within the state, on application of this corporation or of a creditor, shareholder, or member of the corporation, or an application of a receiver appointed for the corporation, may order a meeting of the creditors or class of creditors or of the shareholders or members or class of shareholders or members to be affected by the proposed compromise or arrangement or reorganization, to be summoned in such manner as the court directs. If a majority in number representing 3/4 in value of the creditors or class of creditors, or of the shareholders or members or class of shareholders or members to be affected by the proposed compromise or arrangement or a reorganization, agree to a compromise or arrangement or a reorganization of this corporation as a consequence of the compromise or arrangement, the compromise or arrangement and the reorganization, if sanctioned by the court to which the application has been made, shall be binding on all the creditors or class of creditors, or on all the shareholders or members or class of shareholders or members and also on this corporation.

450.2205 Articles of incorporation; including provision of MCL 450.2204; effect on creditors, shareholders, or members of corporation; administration and enforcement of provision by circuit court; restraining actions and proceedings against corporation; appointment and powers of temporary receiver.

Sec. 205.

(1) When the provision of section 204 is included in the original articles of incorporation of a corporation, all persons who become creditors, shareholders, or members of the corporation are deemed to have become creditors, shareholders, or members subject in all respects to that provision, and it shall be binding upon them.
(2) When that provision is inserted in the articles of a corporation by an amendment of the articles, all persons who become creditors, shareholders, or members of the corporation after the amendment becomes effective are deemed to have become creditors, shareholders, or members subject in all respects to that provision, and it shall be binding upon them.
(3) The circuit court may administer and enforce the provision and restrain, during the process of an action, actions and proceedings against the corporation with respect to which the court so restraining has begun the administration or enforcement of the provision, and appoint a temporary receiver for the corporation and grant the receiver such powers as are deemed proper.

450.2209 Articles of incorporation; additional provisions.

Sec. 209.

The articles of incorporation may contain any provision consistent with any of the following:

(a) A provision regarding the management of the corporation or creating, defining, limiting, or regulating the powers of the corporation, its directors, officers, members, or shareholders, or a class of shareholders or members.
(b) A provision that is required or permitted under this act to be included in the bylaws of the corporation.

(c) A provision that eliminates the personal liability of a volunteer director or volunteer officer to the corporation, its shareholders, or its members for monetary damages for a breach of the director's or officer's fiduciary duty. The provision does not eliminate or limit the liability of a director or officer for any of the following:
    (i) A breach of the director's or officer's duty of loyalty to the corporation, its shareholders, or its members.
    (ii) Acts or omissions not in good faith or that involve intentional misconduct or a knowing violation of law.
    (iii) A violation of section 551(1).
    (iv) A transaction from which the director or officer derived an improper personal benefit.
    (v) An act or omission occurring before the effective date of the provision granting limited liability.
    (vi) An act or omission that is grossly negligent.
(d) For a tax exempt corporation under section 501(c)(3) of the internal revenue code, a provision that the corporation assumes all liability to any person other than the corporation, its shareholders, or its members for all acts or omissions of a volunteer director occurring on or after January 1, 1988 incurred in the good faith performance of the volunteer director's duties.
(e) A provision that a nonprofit corporation assumes the liability for all acts or omissions of a volunteer director, volunteer officer, or other volunteer occurring on or after the effective date of the provision granting limited liability if all of the following are met:
    (i) The volunteer was acting or reasonably believed he or she was acting within the scope of his or her authority.
    (ii) The volunteer was acting in good faith.
    (iii) The volunteer's conduct did not amount to gross negligence or willful and wanton misconduct.
    (iv) The volunteer's conduct was not an intentional tort.
    (v) The volunteer's conduct was not a tort arising out of the ownership, maintenance, or use of a motor vehicle for which tort liability may be imposed as provided in section 3135 of the insurance code of 1956, Act No. 218 of the Public Acts of 1956, being section 500.3135 of the Michigan Compiled Laws.

450.2212 Corporate name.

Sec. 212.

(1) The corporate name of a corporation formed or existing under or subject to this act:
  (a) Shall not contain a word or phrase, or abbreviation or derivative thereof, which indicates or implies that the corporation is organized for a purpose other than 1 or more of the purposes permitted by its articles of incorporation.
  (b) Shall not be the same as, or confusingly similar to, the corporate name of a domestic corporation, a domestic business corporation, a foreign corporation authorized to conduct affairs in this state, or a foreign business corporation authorized to transact business in this state; a corporate name currently reserved under this act, a predecessor act, or Act No. 284 of the Public Acts of 1972, as amended; or a name assumed under section 217 or under section 217 of Act No. 284 of the Public Acts of 1972, as amended, being section 450.1217 of the Michigan Compiled Laws, unless the written consent of the other domestic corporation, domestic business corporation, foreign corporation, or foreign business corporation or holder of a reserved name, to the adoption of a confusingly similar name, but not the same name, is filed in the office of the administrator, or, in lieu of the consent there is filed a certified copy of a final judgment of a court of competent jurisdiction establishing the prior right of the corporation to the use of the name in this state.
  (c) Shall not contain a word or phrase, or an abbreviation or derivative thereof, the use of which is prohibited or restricted by any other statute of this state, unless the restriction has been complied with.
(2) Whenever a foreign corporation is unable to obtain a certificate of authority to conduct affairs in this state because its corporate name does not comply with the provisions of subsection (1), it may apply for authority to conduct affairs in this state by adding to its corporate name in such application a word, abbreviation, or other distinctive and distinguishing element, or alternatively, adopting for use in this state an assumed name otherwise available for use. If in the judgment of the administrator this assumed name would comply with the provisions of subsection (1), that subsection shall not be a bar to the issuance to the corporation of a certificate of authority to conduct affairs in this state. The certificate issued to the foreign corporation shall be issued in this assumed name and the corporation shall use this name in all its dealings with the administrator and in the conduct of its affairs in this state.

(3) A corporation incorporated for the purpose of receiving and administering funds for perpetuation of the memory of persons, preservation of objects of historical or natural interest, educational, charitable, or religious purposes, or public welfare may use the name foundation.

450.2213 Assuming name that implies corporation is banking corporation, insurance or surety company, or trust company prohibited.

Sec. 213.

A corporation formed or existing under or subject to this act shall not assume a name which implies that it is a banking corporation, an insurance or surety company, or a trust company.

450.2215 Reservation of right to use corporate name; application; duration; expiration; extension; transfer of right to exclusive use of reserved corporate name.

Sec. 215.

(1) A person may reserve the right to use of a corporate name by executing and filing an application to reserve the name. If the administrator finds that the name is available for corporate use, the administrator shall reserve it for exclusive use of the applicant for a period expiring at the end of the fourth full calendar month following the month in which the application was filed.
(2) The administrator, for good cause shown, may extend the reservation for periods of not more than 2 calendar months each. Not more than 2 extensions shall be granted.
(3) The right to exclusive use of a corporate name so reserved may be transferred to another person by filing a notice of the transfer, executed by the applicant for whom the name was reserved, and stating the name and address of the transferee.

450.2217 Conduct of affairs under assumed name or names other than corporate name; assumption of same name by 2 or more corporations participating in partnership or joint venture; certificate of assumed name; duration; extensions; notification of impending expiration; substantive rights to use of assumed name not created.

Sec. 217.

Except as otherwise prohibited by law, a domestic or foreign corporation may conduct its affairs under any assumed name or names other than its corporate name, not precluded from use by section 212, and the same name may be assumed by 2 or more corporations participating together in any partnership or joint venture by filing a certificate stating the true name of the corporation and the assumed name under which its affairs are to be conducted. The certificate shall be effective, unless sooner terminated by the filing of a certificate of termination or by the dissolution or withdrawal of the corporation, for a period expiring on December 31 of the fifth full calendar year following the year in which it was filed. It may be extended for additional consecutive periods of 5 full calendar years each by the filing of similar certificates not earlier than 90 days preceding the expiration of any such period. The administrator shall notify the corporation of the impending expiration of the certificate of assumed name no later than 90 days before the initial or subsequent 5-year period will expire. This section does not create substantive rights to the use of a particular assumed name.

450.2221 Corporate existence to begin on effective date of articles; filing as conclusive evidence that conditions precedent fulfilled and corporation organized; exception.

Sec. 221.

The corporate existence shall begin on the effective date of the articles of incorporation as provided in section 131. Filing is conclusive evidence that all conditions precedent required to be performed under this act have been fulfilled and that the corporation has been organized under this act, except in an action or special proceeding by the attorney general.

450.2223 Selection of board and adoption of bylaws; first meeting; notice; quorum; transaction of business.

Sec. 223.

Before or after filing of the articles of incorporation a majority of the incorporators at a meeting or by written instrument, shall select a board and may adopt bylaws. On or after the filing date of the articles, any member of the board may call the first meeting of the board upon not less than 3 days' notice by mail to each director. A majority of the directors constitutes a quorum for the first meeting of the board. At the first meeting, the board may adopt bylaws, elect officers, and transact such other business as may come before the meeting.

450.2231 Bylaws; adoption; amendment or repeal; contents.

Sec. 231.

(1) Except if the power to adopt, amend, or repeal the bylaws is reserved exclusively to the corporation's shareholders, its members, or its board in the articles of incorporation:
   (a) The initial bylaws of a corporation shall be adopted by its incorporators, its shareholders, its members, or its board.
   (b) The shareholders, the members, or the board may amend or repeal the bylaws or adopt new bylaws.
   (c) The shareholders or members may prescribe in the bylaws that any bylaw adopted by them shall not be amended or repealed by the board.
(2) The bylaws may contain any provision for the regulation and management of the affairs of the corporation not inconsistent with law or the articles of incorporation.

450.2241 Registered office; resident agent.

Sec. 241.

Each domestic corporation and each foreign corporation authorized to conduct affairs in this state shall have and continuously maintain in this state:
(a) A registered office which may be the same as its place of business.
(b) A resident agent, which agent may be either an individual resident in this state whose business office is identical with the corporation's registered office, a domestic or domestic business corporation, or a foreign or foreign business corporation authorized to conduct affairs or transact business in this state and having a business office identical with the corporation's registered office.

450.2242 Change of registered office or resident agent; statement.

Sec. 242.

A domestic corporation or a foreign corporation authorized to conduct affairs in this state may change its registered office or change its resident agent, or both, upon filing a statement, which may be executed by any of the individuals set forth in section 132 or by the secretary or assistant secretary of the corporation, setting forth:

(a) The name of the corporation.
(b) The street address of its then registered office, and its mailing address if different from its street address.
(c) If the address of its registered office is changed, the street address and the mailing address, if different from the street address, to which the registered office is to be changed.
(d) The name of its then resident agent.
(e) If its resident agent is changed, the name of its successor resident agent.
(f) That the address of its registered office and the address of the business office of its resident agent, as changed, will be identical.
(g) That such change was authorized by resolution duly adopted by its board.

450.2243 Resident agent; resignation; notice; appointment of successor; termination of appointment of resigning agent.

Sec. 243.

A resident agent of a domestic or foreign corporation may resign by filing a written notice of resignation with the president or a vice-president of the corporation and with the administrator. The corporation shall promptly appoint a successor resident agent. The appointment of the resigning agent terminates upon appointment of a successor or upon expiration of 30 days after receipt of the notice by the administrator, whichever first occurs.

450.2246 Resident agent; service of process, notice, or demand; resident agent as agent of director or officer in certain actions; forwarding process to director or officer.

Sec. 246.

(1) The resident agent so appointed by a corporation is an agent of the corporation upon whom any process, notice, or demand required or permitted by law to be served upon the corporation may be served.

(2) A person, whether a resident or nonresident of this state, by acceptance of election, appointment, or employment as a director or officer of a corporation organized under this act or in existence on the effective date of this act, by such acceptance is held to have appointed the resident agent of the corporation as the person's agent upon whom process may be served while the person is a director or officer, in any action commenced in a court of general jurisdiction in this state, arising out of or founded upon any action of such a domestic corporation or of such person as a director or officer of the domestic corporation. Upon accepting service of process, the resident agent shall promptly forward it to the director or officer at the director or officer's last known address.

450.2251 Corporate purposes; conduct of lawful activities during war or national emergency.

Sec. 251.

(1) Except if required by law to incorporate under another statute of this state, a corporation may be formed under this act for any lawful purposes not involving pecuniary gain or profit for its officers, directors, shareholders, or members.
(2) In time of war or other national emergency, a corporation may conduct any lawful activity, including any business activity, in aid thereof, notwithstanding the purposes set forth in its articles of incorporation, at the request or direction of a competent governmental authority.

450.2261 Corporate powers; inconsistency between certain acts; fixed limitation or term; waiver of right to perpetual existence; nonprofit power corporation.

Sec. 261.

(1) A corporation, subject to any limitation provided in this act, in any other statute of this state, in its articles of incorporation, or otherwise by law, has the power in furtherance of its corporate purposes to do any of the following:
   (a) Have perpetual duration.
   (b) Sue and be sued in all courts and participate in actions and proceedings judicial, administrative, arbitrative, or otherwise, in the same manner as a natural person.

(c) Have a corporate seal, and alter the seal, and use it by causing it or a facsimile to be affixed, impressed, or reproduced in any other manner.
(d) Adopt, amend, or repeal bylaws, including emergency bylaws, relating to the purposes of the corporation, the conduct of its affairs, its rights and powers, and the rights and powers of its shareholders, members, directors, or officers.
(e) Elect or appoint officers, employees, and other agents of the corporation, prescribe their duties, fix their compensation and the compensation of directors, and indemnify corporate directors, officers, employees, and agents.
(f) Purchase, receive, take by grant, gift, devise, bequest, or otherwise, lease, or otherwise acquire, own, hold, improve, employ, use, and otherwise deal in and with, real or personal property, or an interest in real or personal property, wherever situated, either absolutely or in trust and without limitation as to amount or value.
(g) Sell, convey, lease, exchange, transfer, or otherwise dispose of, or mortgage or pledge, or create a security interest in, any of its property, or an interest in the property, wherever situated.
(h) Purchase, take, receive, subscribe for, or otherwise acquire, own, hold, vote, employ, sell, lend, lease, exchange, transfer, or otherwise dispose of, mortgage, pledge, use, and otherwise deal in and with, bonds and other obligations, shares or other securities or interests or memberships issued by others, whether engaged in similar or different business, governmental, or other activities, including banking corporations or trust companies. A corporation organized or conducting affairs in this state under this act shall not guarantee or become surety upon a bond or other undertaking securing the deposit of public money.
(i) Make contracts, give guarantees, and incur liabilities, borrow money at such rates of interest as the corporation may determine, issue its notes, bonds, and other obligations, and secure any of its obligations by mortgage or pledge of any of its property or an interest in the property, wherever situated.
(j) Lend money, invest and reinvest its funds, and take and hold real and personal property as security for the payment of funds loaned or invested.
(k) Make donations for public welfare or for community fund, hospital, charitable, educational, scientific, civic, or similar purposes, and in

time of war or other national emergency in aid of war or other national emergency.
(l) Pay pensions, establish and carry out pension, savings, thrift, and other retirement, incentive, and benefit plans, trusts and provisions for any of its directors, officers, and employees.
(m) Purchase, receive, take, otherwise acquire, own, hold, sell, lend, exchange, transfer, otherwise dispose of, pledge, use, and otherwise deal in and with its own shares, bonds, and other securities.
(n) Participate with others in any corporation, business corporation, partnership, limited partnership, joint venture, or other association of any kind, or participate with others in any transaction, undertaking, or agreement that the participating corporation would have power to conduct by itself, whether or not the participation involves sharing or delegation of control with or to others.
(o) Cease its corporate activities and dissolve.
(p) Conduct its affairs, carry on its operations, and have offices and exercise the powers granted by this act in any jurisdiction within or without the United States, and, in the case of a corporation the purpose or purposes of which require the transaction of business, the receipt and payment of money, the care and custody of property, and other incidental business matters, transact such business, receive, collect, and disburse such money, and engage in such other incidental business matters as are naturally or properly within the scope of its articles.
(q) Have and exercise all powers necessary or convenient to effect any purpose for which the corporation is formed.
(2) A corporation subject to the uniform prudent management of institutional funds act has all powers granted under both this act and that act. However, in the event of an inconsistency between the 2 acts, the uniform prudent management of institutional funds act controls.
(3) The corporate existence of all corporations incorporated before January 1, 1983, without capital stock, for religious, benevolent, social, or fraternal purposes, shall be considered to be in perpetuity. A limitation or term fixed in the articles or in the law under which the corporation originally incorporated is not effective unless the corporation affirmatively waived its right to perpetual existence after September 18, 1931, by fixing a definite term of existence by amendment to its articles.
(4) Any nonprofit power corporation that is authorized to furnish electric service may construct, maintain, and operate its lines along, over, across, or under any public places, streets, and highways, and across or under

the waters in this state, with all necessary erections and fixtures. A nonprofit power corporation may exercise the power of eminent domain, in the manner provided by the uniform condemnation procedures act, 1980 PA 87, MCL 213.51 to 213.75. As a condition to the exercise of any of these powers, nonprofit corporations are subject to the jurisdiction of the Michigan public service commission pursuant to 1909 PA 106, MCL 460.551 to 460.559, 1919 PA 419, MCL 460.54 to 460.62, and 1939 PA 3, MCL 460.1 to 460.11.

450.2262 Existing incorporated association or society operating as corporation subject to act; payment of death or sick benefits; reserves; rules; investment of funds securing reserves; statement required of evidence of obligation to pay death and sick benefits.

Sec. 262.

(1) An association or society, not otherwise provided for here or by other statute, incorporated before January 1, 1983, and now existing, whose purpose is to provide for the relief of distressed members, visitation of the sick, and the payment of a voluntary sick benefit to or for members not exceeding $2,000.00 on account of any 1 member, or the buying and selling of products for its members without direct pecuniary profit to the association or its members may operate as a corporation subject to this act. The ladies Lutheran benevolent federation of Michigan, now incorporated as a nonprofit corporation, may pay death benefits in an amount not exceeding $500.00 to any 1 person. The metropolitan club of America, inc., national spirit, and the ladies auxiliary of the metropolitan clubs of America, national spirit, which are incorporated as nonprofit corporations, may pay death benefits in an amount not to exceed $1,000.00 to any 1 person. The Venetian club of mutual aid, incorporated as a nonprofit corporation, may pay death and sick benefits in an amount not to exceed $10,000.00 to any 1 person. The Warren firemen's benevolent association may pay death and sick benefits in an amount not to exceed $20,000.00 to any 1 person. The Lansing firemen's benefit association may pay death and sick benefits in an amount not to exceed $2,000.00 to any 1 person. The Sanilac county police and firemen's fund may pay death and sick benefits in an amount not to exceed $3,000.00 to any 1 person. The Italian-American brotherhood society may pay death and sick benefits in an amount not to exceed $3,000.00 to any 1 person. The Italian-American fraternal club of

Dearborn may pay death and sick benefits in an amount not to exceed $500.00 to any 1 person. The Michigan licensed beverage association may pay death and sick benefits in an amount not to exceed $5,000.00 to any 1 person who is a licensee of the Michigan liquor control commission. The Westland fire fighters' benevolent association may pay death and sick benefits in an amount not to exceed $7,500.00 to any 1 person. The Livonia benevolent association for fire fighters and police officers may pay death and sick benefits in an amount not to exceed $5,000.00 to any 1 person. The Midland fire fighters' benefit fund may pay death and sick benefits in an amount not to exceed $10,000.00 to any 1 person. The incorporated branches of the fraternal order of eagles within this state may pay death benefits of $350.00 or sickness benefits of $350.00, but not a combination of death and sickness benefits that would exceed $500.00 to any 1 person.

(2) The entities specified in this section and organized before January 1, 1983, and providing for the payment of death or sick benefits under this section in an amount exceeding $1,000.00 to 1 person shall by January 1, 1980, establish and maintain reserves in an amount estimated in the aggregate to provide for the payment of all losses and claims incurred, whether reported or unreported, which are unpaid and for which the entity may be liable and to provide for the expense of adjustment or settlement of losses and claims. The reserves shall be computed in accordance with rules promulgated by the commissioner of insurance, after due notice and hearing, upon reasonable consideration of the ascertained experiences and the character of such kinds of business for the purpose of adequately protecting the members and securing the solvency of the corporations. The funds of the entities securing the reserves shall be invested only in securities permitted by the laws of this state for the investment of assets of life insurance companies.

(3) An entity specified in this section that obligates itself to the payment of death and sick benefits to its members shall not make, issue, or deliver in this state a certificate or other written evidence of the obligation unless the certificate or other written evidence has conspicuously printed on the first page in boldface type not smaller than 10 point the following statement: This organization does not operate under the supervision of the Michigan insurance bureau.

450.2271 Act of corporation and transfer of property to or by corporation not invalid where corporation without capacity or power; assertion of lack of capacity or power.

Sec. 271.

An act of a corporation and a transfer of real or personal property to or by a corporation, otherwise lawful, is not invalid because the corporation was without capacity or power to do the act or make or receive the transfer of property. However the lack of capacity or power may be asserted:
(a) By a shareholder or member, or by a director who has not authorized or consented to the act or transfer, in an action against the corporation to enjoin the doing of an act or the transfer of real or personal property by or to the corporation.
(b) In an action by or in the right of the corporation to procure a judgment in its favor against an incumbent or former officer or director of the corporation for loss or damage due to an unauthorized act by that person.
(c) In an action or special proceeding by the attorney general to dissolve the corporation or to enjoin it from the conducting of unauthorized affairs.

450.2275 Agreement to pay rate of interest in excess of legal rate; defense of usury prohibited.

Sec. 275.

A domestic or foreign corporation, whether or not formed at the request of a lender, may by agreement in writing, and not otherwise, agree to pay a rate of interest in excess of the legal rate and in such case the defense of usury is prohibited.

Chapter 3 – Structure

450.2301 Payment or distribution of assets, income, or profit; conferring benefits on shareholders or members; compensation; distribution of assets upon dissolution; providing for payment of dividends or distribution of income or profit in articles or bylaws; application or distribution of profits; use, conveyance, or distribution of assets held by corporation for charitable purposes.

Sec. 301.

(1) A payment or distribution of any part of the assets, income, or profit of a corporation shall be in conformity with the purposes of the corporation.
(2) A corporation may confer benefits on its shareholders or members in conformity with the purposes of the corporation.
(3) A corporation shall not pay dividends or distribute any part of its assets, income, or profit to its shareholders, members, directors, or officers, except as follows:
 (a) A corporation may pay compensation in a reasonable amount to shareholders, members, directors, or officers for services rendered to the corporation.
 (b) Upon dissolution as permitted by this act, a corporation may make distributions of assets, other than assets held for charitable purposes, to shareholders or members.
 (c) The articles of incorporation or bylaws of a corporation whose purposes include providing a benefit to its member or shareholder corporation may provide that the corporation may pay dividends or distribute its income or profit to its member or shareholder corporation.
 (d) As permitted in subsection (4).
 (e) If provision for redemption of shares is made pursuant to sections 361 to 365.
(4) A corporation whose lawful activities include the charging of fees or prices for its services or products may receive the income and may make a profit as a result of its receipt. All such resulting profit shall be applied to the maintenance, expansion, or operation of the lawful activities of the corporation and shall not be distributed to the shareholders, members, directors, or officers of the corporation. However, profit derived solely from the charging of fees or prices by a corporation to its shareholders or members for its services or products may be distributed to the

shareholders or members on the basis of, or in proportion to, the fees or prices paid by shareholders or members to the corporation for its services or products.

(5) This act shall not be deemed to permit assets held by a corporation for charitable purposes to be used, conveyed or distributed for noncharitable purposes.

450.2302 Corporation organized upon nonstock basis.

Sec. 302.

A corporation shall be organized upon a stock or nonstock basis. A corporation organized upon a nonstock basis shall be organized upon a membership basis or a directorship basis.

450.2303 Corporation organized upon stock basis; provisions of articles and bylaws; issuance of shares; rights, preferences, and limitations of or upon shareholders; classes of shares; voting rights; transferability and cancellation of shares; rules of qualification and government.

Sec. 303.

(1) A corporation organized upon a stock basis may issue the number of shares authorized in its articles of incorporation. Except as otherwise provided in this act, the articles of incorporation or bylaws may prescribe the qualifications, liquidation rights, preferences, and limitations, and other rights, preferences, and limitations of or upon the shareholders of the corporation.

(2) The articles of incorporation may provide that the shares of a corporation shall be all of 1 class or shall be divided into 2 or more classes. If the shares are divided into 2 or more classes, the shares of each class shall be designated to distinguish them from the shares of the other classes. Except as otherwise provided in this act, each class shall consist of shares of the designation and number stated in the articles of incorporation, and having relative qualifications, liquidation rights, preferences, and limitations, and other rights, preferences, and limitations as may be stated in the articles of incorporation or the bylaws. Each share shall be equal to every other share of the same class.

(3) Each shareholder shall have 1 vote for each share of stock held by that shareholder on each matter submitted to a vote of shareholders, unless

the articles or bylaws provide that each shareholder shall have 1 vote regardless of shares held by that shareholder or unless the articles or bylaws deny, limit, or otherwise prescribe the voting rights of shares of any class. The shareholders and each affected class of shareholders, if any, shall adopt, amend, or repeal any bylaw denying, limiting, or otherwise prescribing the voting rights of shareholders or any class of shareholders.

(4) Except as otherwise provided by the articles or bylaws, shares of stock shall not be transferable and shall be canceled upon the death or resignation of the owner of the shares.

(5) A corporation may adopt rules of qualification and government of its shareholders pursuant to its articles and bylaws. Adopted rules shall be reasonable, germane to the purposes of the corporation, and equally enforced as to all shareholders. A corporation may provide for the cancellation of the stock of a shareholder who fails to comply with adopted rules without liability for an accounting.

450.2304 Corporation organized upon membership basis; provisions of articles or bylaws; rights, preferences, and limitations of or upon members; classes of members; voting rights; condominium association; homeowners or property owners association; transferability and termination of membership; rules of qualification and government; limitations on membership.

Sec. 304.

(1) Except as otherwise provided in this act, the articles of incorporation or bylaws of a corporation organized upon a membership basis may prescribe the number, qualifications, liquidation rights, preferences, and limitations, and other rights, preferences, and limitations of or upon the members of the corporation.

(2) A corporation organized upon a membership basis may have 1 or more classes of members. Except as otherwise provided in this act, any provision for classes of members and the relative number, qualifications, liquidation rights, preferences, and limitations, and other rights, preferences, and limitations of or upon each class shall be set forth in the articles of incorporation or the bylaws. Each member of any class of members shall have equal rights with all members of that class.

(3) Each member of a corporation, regardless of class, shall be entitled to 1 vote on each matter submitted to a vote of members, unless the articles or bylaws deny, limit, or otherwise prescribe the voting rights of any class of members. The members and each affected class of members, if any, shall adopt, amend, or repeal any bylaw denying, limiting, or otherwise prescribing the voting rights of any class of members.

(4) Members of a condominium association formed for the purposes of administering the affairs of a condominium project are entitled to voting rights as designated by the master deed of the condominium.

(5) The articles of incorporation or the bylaws may provide that members of a homeowners or property owners association are entitled to voting rights predicated on the number of lots owned by each member.

(6) Except as otherwise provided in this act, the articles of incorporation or the bylaws, membership shall not be transferable and shall be terminated by death, resignation, expulsion, or expiration of a term of membership.

(7) A corporation may adopt rules of qualification and government of its members, including rules of admission to, retention of, and expulsion from membership, pursuant to its articles and bylaws. Such rules shall be reasonable, germane to the purposes of the corporation, and equally enforced as to all members.

(8) The articles of incorporation of a corporation organized upon a membership basis may provide that membership shall be limited to persons who are members in good standing in other corporations. The articles of incorporation may provide that failure to remain a member in good standing in the other corporation constitutes grounds for expulsion of a member if the bylaws of the corporation prescribe the nature of the evidence and the procedures for expulsion which shall be followed.

450.2305 Corporation organized upon directorship basis; members; voting; matters subject to action by board of directors.

Sec. 305.

(1) A corporation organized upon a directorship basis may or may not have members. If a corporation organized upon a directorship basis has members, the members shall not be entitled to vote.

(2) Unless the context of a provision of this act otherwise requires, all matters which are subject to membership vote or other action in this act in the case of a membership corporation shall be subject to duly authorized action by the board of directors of a directorship corporation.

450.2307 Subscription for shares or membership; enforceability; irrevocability; acceptance; consent to revocation; contract with corporation to purchase shares to be issued or treasury shares as subscription agreement.

Sec. 307.

(1) A subscription for shares or membership made before or after organization of a corporation is not enforceable unless in writing and signed by the subscriber.
(2) A subscription for shares of or membership in a corporation to be organized may provide that it is irrevocable and may be accepted by the corporation for a period of 6 months, unless all the subscribers consent to its revocation.
(3) A contract with a corporation to purchase its shares to be issued or its treasury shares is a subscription agreement and not an executory contract to purchase shares, unless otherwise provided in the contract.

450.2308 Subscription for shares or membership; payment; installments; call for payment ratable; retention of shares as security for performance by subscriber.

Sec. 308.

Unless otherwise provided in the subscription agreement:
(a) A subscription for shares or for membership made before or after organization of a corporation, shall be paid in full at such time, or in such installments and at such times, as shall be determined by the board.
(b) A call made by the board for payment on subscriptions shall be ratable as to all shares or members of the same class.
(c) A corporation may retain any shares as security for performance by the subscriber of the subscriber's obligations under a subscription agreement and subject to the power of sale or rescission upon default provided in section 309.

450.2309 Default in payment of amount due under subscription agreement; rights and duties of corporation; interpretation; limiting and adding to rights and remedies of corporation.

Sec. 309.

(1) In case of default in payment of an installment or call or other amount due under a subscription agreement, including an amount which may become due as a result of a default in performance of any provision thereof, the corporation has the following rights and duties:
   (a) It may collect the amount due in the same manner as any other debt owing to it.
   (b) If the articles of incorporation or bylaws of a corporation organized upon a stock basis permit the transfer of shares, it may sell the shares in any reasonable manner consistent therewith at any time before full satisfaction of the claim or a judgment therefor. Notice of the time and place of a public sale or of the time after which a private sale may be had, together with a statement of the amount due upon each share, shall be given in writing to the subscriber personally or by registered or certified mail at least 20 days before any such time stated in the notice. Any excess of net proceeds realized over the amount due plus interest shall be paid to the subscriber. If the sale is made in good faith, in a reasonable manner, and upon such notice, the corporation may recover the difference between the amount due plus interest and the net proceeds of the sale. A good faith purchaser for value acquires title to the sold shares free of any right of the subscriber even though the corporation fails to comply with 1 or more of the requirements of this subdivision.
   (c) It may rescind the subscription, with the effect provided in section 310, and may recover damages for breach of contract. In the case of transferable shares of a corporation organized upon a stock basis, unless special circumstances show proximate damages of a different amount, the measure of damages shall be the difference between the market price at the time and place of tender of the shares and the unpaid contract price. Liquidated damages may be provided for in the subscription agreement in any amount which is reasonable, including the difficulties of proof of loss. The subscriber may have restitution of the amount by which the sum of payments exceeds the corporation's damages for breach of contract, whether fixed by agreement or judgment.

(2) The rights and duties set forth in this section shall be interpreted as cumulative so far as is consistent with entitling the corporation to a full and single recovery of the amount due or its damages. The subscription

agreement may limit the rights and remedies of the corporation set forth in this section, and may add to them so far as is consistent with this subsection.

450.2310 Rescission of subscription under which part of shares issued and in which security interest retained as cancellation of shares.

Sec. 310.

Rescission by a corporation of a subscription under which a part of the shares subscribed for have been issued and in which the corporation retains a security interest, as provided in section 308(c), effects the cancellation of such shares.

450.2311 Fees or dues required as condition of shareholding or membership; fixing; enforcement.

Sec. 311.

A corporation may fix in the bylaws, or the bylaws may authorize the board to fix, an amount as fees or dues which shareholders or members may be required to pay initially or periodically as a condition of shareholding or admission or retention of membership. The corporation may make bylaws necessary to enforce this requirement, including provisions for cancellation of shares or termination of membership for nonpayment of dues or obligations and for reissuance of shares or reinstatement of membership.

450.2312 Issuance by corporation organized on stock basis of shares for fixed consideration; disposition of treasury shares.

Sec. 312.

(1) Shares may be issued by a corporation organized on a stock basis for a consideration fixed by the board unless the articles of incorporation reserve this right to the shareholders.
(2) Unless otherwise provided in the articles of incorporation, treasury shares which are transferable may be disposed of by the corporation for a consideration fixed by the board.

450.2313 Corporation, unincorporated association, partnership, or other person as shareholder or member; officers and directors as director of

corporation; rights, powers, privileges, and liabilities of shareholders or members.

Sec. 313.

(1) Except as otherwise provided in the articles of incorporation or the bylaws, corporations, business corporations, unincorporated associations, and partnerships and any other person without limitation, may be a shareholder or a member of a corporation.
(2) If a corporation or business corporation is a shareholder or a member in a corporation, its officers or directors may serve as a director of the corporation of which it is a shareholder or member. A corporation or business corporation that is also a shareholder or member of a corporation shall possess and exercise all the rights, powers, privileges, and liabilities of individual shareholders or members.

450.2315 Consideration for issuance of shares; rights and privileges of subscribers when payment received by corporation; value of consideration; fully paid shares nonassessable.

Sec. 315.

(1) The consideration for the issuance of shares may be paid, in whole or in part, in money or other property, tangible or intangible, or in services performed or to be performed for the corporation or for its benefit or in its organization or reorganization.
(2) Except where the consideration is future services or payment, when payment of the full consideration for which shares are to be issued is received by the corporation, the subscriber has all the rights and privileges of a holder of such shares, including registration in the subscriber's name of a certificate representing them; and the shares shall be fully paid. Where the consideration is future services or payment, rights of the subscriber shall be determined by the subscription agreement.
(3) In the absence of fraud in the transaction, the judgment of the board of the shareholders as to the value of the consideration received for shares is conclusive.
(4) Unless the articles of incorporation otherwise provide, shares which are fully paid shall be nonassessable.

450.2317 Obligation to pay unpaid portion of consideration for shares or membership as sole obligation; liability of person holding stock or membership in fiduciary or representative capacity; liability of assignee, transferee, or pledgee of shares, membership, or subscription for unpaid portion of consideration.

Sec. 317.

(1) A holder of or subscriber for shares or membership of a corporation is under no obligation to the corporation or its creditors to pay for the shares or membership other than the obligation to pay to the corporation the unpaid portion of the consideration for which the shares were issued or to be issued or the membership was granted or to be granted.
(2) A person holding stock or membership in a fiduciary or representative capacity is not personally liable to the corporation as the holder of or subscriber for shares or membership of a corporation, but the estate and funds in the person's hands are so liable.
(3) A person becoming an assignee, transferee, or pledgee of shares or membership or of a subscription for shares or membership in good faith and without knowledge or notice that the full consideration therefor has not been paid is not liable to the corporation or its creditors for any unpaid portion of the consideration, but the original holder or subscriber and any assignee or transferee before an assignment or transfer to a person taking in good faith and without knowledge or notice remains liable therefor.

450.2327 Charges and expenses of organization or reorganization; sale or underwriting expenses and compensation; payment or allowance.

Sec. 327.

The reasonable charges and expenses of organization or reorganization of a corporation, and the reasonable expenses of and compensation for the sale or underwriting of its shares, may be paid or allowed by the corporation out of the consideration received by it in payment for its shares without thereby rendering the shares not fully paid or assessable.

450.2331 Representation of shares by certificates; signatures of officers and seal.

Sec. 331.

The shares of a corporation shall be represented by certificates signed by the chairperson of the board, vice-chairperson of the board, president, vice-president, treasurer, or other officer authorized by the bylaws or a resolution of the board, and may be sealed with the seal of the corporation or a facsimile thereof. The signatures of the officers may be facsimile if the certificate is countersigned by a transfer agent or registered by a registrar other than the corporation itself or its employee. In case an officer who has signed or whose facsimile signature has been placed upon a certificate ceases to be an officer before the certificate is issued, it may be issued by the corporation with the same effect as if the person were an officer at the date of issue.

450.2332 Certificate representing shares; required statements.

Sec. 332.

(1) A certificate representing shares shall state upon its face:
    (a) That the corporation is a nonprofit corporation formed under the laws of this state.
    (b) The name of the person to whom issued.
    (c) The number and class of shares which the certificate represents.
    (d) A statement that the shares are not transferable, unless the articles or bylaws provide that shares shall be transferable, in which case the certificate shall state any conditions or limitations on transferability of the shares.
    (e) The act under which the corporation was formed.
(2) A certificate representing shares issued by a corporation which is authorized to issue shares of more than 1 class shall set forth on its face or back or state that the corporation will furnish to a shareholder upon request and without charge a full statement of the designation, relative rights, preferences, and limitations of the shares of each class authorized to be issued.

450.2334 Lost or destroyed certificate; issuance of new certificate; bond.

Sec. 334.

A corporation may issue a new certificate for shares or fractional shares in place of a certificate theretofore issued by it, alleged to have been lost or destroyed, and the board may require the owner of the lost or destroyed certificate, or the owner's legal representative, to give the corporation a bond sufficient to indemnify the corporation against any claim that may be made against it on account of the alleged lost or destroyed certificate or the issuance of such a new certificate.

450.2338 Issuing certificates for fractions of share; purposes; rights of holders; paying fair value of fractions of share in cash; issuing scrip in registered or bearer form exchangeable for full shares; conditions; providing opportunity to purchase additional fractions of share or scrip.

Sec. 338.

(1) A corporation may issue certificates for fractions of a share where necessary to effect share transfer, share distributions, or a reclassification, merger, consolidation, or reorganization, which shall entitle the holders, in proportion to their fractional holdings, to exercise voting rights and participate in liquidating distributions.

(2) As an alternative, a corporation may pay in cash the fair value of fractions of a share as of the time when those entitled to receive the fractions are determined.

(3) As an alternative, a corporation may issue scrip in registered or bearer form over the manual or facsimile signature of an officer of the corporation or of its agent, exchangeable as therein provided for full shares, but such scrip shall not entitle the holder to any right of a shareholder except as therein provided. The scrip shall be issued subject to the condition that it becomes void if not exchanged for certificates representing full shares before a specified date. The scrip may be subject to the condition that the shares for which the scrip is exchangeable may be sold by the corporation and the proceeds of the sale distributed to the holders of the scrip, or subject to any other condition which the board may determine.

(4) A corporation may provide reasonable opportunity for persons entitled to fractions of a share or scrip to sell them or to purchase additional fractions of a share or scrip needed to acquire a full share.

450.2361 Shares redeemable upon occurrence of specified event or events in cash, bonds, or other property; classes; sinking fund for redemption.

Sec. 361.

A corporation may provide in its articles of incorporation for 1 or more classes of shares which are redeemable, in whole or in part, upon the occurrence of a specified event or events in cash, its bonds or other property at such prices, within such periods, and under such conditions as are stated in the articles, if the provision for redemption is consistent with the purpose or purposes of the corporation. If so provided in its articles, a corporation may create a sinking fund for redemption, in whole or in part, of any class of redeemable shares.

450.2363 Shares redeemable at option of shareholders in cash, bonds, or other property; classes; amendment to articles.

Sec. 363.

A corporation may provide, in its original articles of incorporation or by an amendment approved by the holders of record of all outstanding shares, for 1 or more classes of shares which are redeemable, in whole or in part, at the option of the shareholders, if the provision for redemption is consistent with the purpose or purposes of the corporation. Subject to restrictions imposed by section 365, such shares may be redeemable in cash, bonds of the corporation, or other property, at such prices within such periods, and under such conditions as are stated in the articles. The articles may be amended to delete or change a provision for shares redeemable at the option of the shareholder only with unanimous approval of the holders of such shares.

450.2365 Purchase or redemption by corporation of own shares under certain conditions prohibited.

Sec. 365.

A corporation shall not purchase or redeem its own shares under any of the following conditions:
(a) If the purchase or redemption is inconsistent with the purpose or purposes of the corporation.
(b) If the purchase or redemption is contrary to any restriction contained in the articles of incorporation.
(c) When the corporation is insolvent or when the purchase or redemption would render the corporation insolvent.
(d) Unless after purchase or redemption there remains outstanding 1 or more classes of shares possessing, among them collectively, voting rights.

(e) In the case of redeemable shares and within the period of their redeemability, at a price greater than the applicable redemption price.
(f) Contrary to section 301(5).

450.2371 Cancellation of shares reacquired by corporation; retention of reacquired shares as treasury shares; status of cancelled shares.

Sec. 371.

(1) Shares that have been issued and have been purchased, redeemed, or otherwise reacquired by a corporation shall be canceled unless the articles of incorporation or bylaws otherwise provide.
(2) Shares reacquired by a corporation and not required to be canceled may be retained as treasury shares or canceled by the board at the time of reacquisition or at any time thereafter.
(3) Shares canceled under this section are restored to the status of authorized but unissued shares. However, if the articles of incorporation or bylaws prohibit reissue of any shares required or permitted to be canceled under this section, the board by resolution shall adopt and file an amendment of the articles reducing the number of authorized shares accordingly.

450.2391 Conferring voting and inspection rights upon bond holders; signatures of officers.

Sec. 391.

(1) A corporation, in its articles of incorporation, may confer upon the holders of bonds issued or to be issued by it, rights to inspect the corporate books and records and to vote in the election of directors and on any other matters on which shareholders or members of the corporation may vote to the extent, in the manner, and subject to the conditions prescribed in the articles. The articles may grant to the board the power to confer such voting or inspection rights under the terms of any bonds issued or to be issued by the corporation.
(2) The signatures of the officers upon a bond may be facsimiles.

Chapter 4 – Meetings

450.2401 Meetings of shareholders or members; location.

Sec. 401.

Meetings of shareholders or members may be held at a place within or without this state as provided in the bylaws. In the absence of such a provision, meetings shall be held at the registered office or such other place as may be determined by the board.

450.2402 Annual meeting of shareholders or members for election of directors and other business; failure to hold meeting at designated time or elect sufficient number of directors; adjournment of meeting; court order to hold meeting or election; quorum.

Sec. 402.

An annual meeting of shareholders or members for election of directors and for such other business as may come before the meeting shall be held at a time as provided in the bylaws, unless such action is taken by written consent as provided in section 407. Failure to hold the annual meeting at the designated time, or to elect a sufficient number of directors at the meeting or any adjournment of the meeting, does not affect otherwise valid corporate acts or work a forfeiture or give cause for dissolution of the corporation, except as provided in section 823. If the annual meeting is not held on the date designated therefor, the board shall cause the meeting to be held as soon thereafter as convenient. If the annual meeting is not held for 90 days after the date designated therefor, or if no date has been designated for 15 months after organization of the corporation or after its last annual meeting, the circuit court for the county in which the registered office of the corporation is located, upon application of a shareholder or member, may summarily order the meeting or the election, or both, to be held at such time and place, upon such notice, and for the transaction of such business as may be designated in the order. At any such meeting ordered to be called by the court, the shareholders or members, present in person or by proxy and having voting powers, constitute a quorum for transaction of the business designated in the order.

450.2403 Special meeting of shareholders or members; court order; quorum.

Sec. 403.

A special meeting of shareholders or members may be called by the board, or by officers, directors, shareholders, or members as provided in the bylaws. Notwithstanding any such provision, upon application of the holders of not less than 10% of all the shares or of not less than 10% of all the members entitled to vote at a meeting, the circuit court for the county in which the registered office is located, for good cause shown, may order a special meeting of shareholders or members to be called and held at such time and place, upon such notice and for the transaction of such business as may be designated in the order. At any such meeting ordered to be called by the court, the shareholders or members present in person or by proxy and having voting powers constitute a quorum for transaction of the business designated in the order.

450.2404 Notice of time, place, and purposes of meeting of shareholders or members; manner; notice of adjourned meeting; notice not given; attendance at meeting as waiver of notice; participating and voting by remote communication.

Sec. 404.

(1) Except as otherwise provided in this act, notice of the time, place, if any, and purposes of a meeting of shareholders or members shall be given in any of the following manners:
   (a) By written notice, given personally, by mail, or by electronic transmission, not less than 10 nor more than 60 days before the date of the meeting to each shareholder or member of record entitled to vote at the meeting.
   (b) By including the notice, prominently displayed, in a newspaper or other periodical regularly published at least semiannually by or in behalf of the corporation and addressed and mailed, postage prepaid, to a member or shareholder entitled to vote at the meeting not less than 10 nor more than 60 days before the meeting.
(2) If a meeting of the shareholders or members is adjourned to another time or place, it is not necessary, unless the bylaws otherwise provide, to give notice of the adjourned meeting if the time and place to which the meeting is adjourned are announced at the meeting at which the adjournment is taken. If after the adjournment the board fixes a new

record date for the adjourned meeting, a notice of the adjourned meeting shall be given to each shareholder or member of record on the new record date entitled to notice under subsection (1).

(3) If a meeting of shareholders or members is adjourned under subsection (2), only business that might have been transacted at the original meeting may be transacted at the adjourned meeting if a notice of the adjourned meeting is not given.

(4) Attendance of a person at a meeting of shareholders or members, in person or by proxy, constitutes a waiver of objection to lack of notice or defective notice of the meeting, unless the shareholder or member at the beginning of the meeting objects to holding the meeting or transacting business at the meeting.

(5) If a shareholder or member is permitted to participate in and vote at a meeting by remote communication under section 405, the notice described in subsection (1) shall include a description of the means of remote communication by which a shareholder or member may participate.

450.2405 Shareholder or member participation in meeting by conference telephone or other means of remote communication; conditions; participation as presence in person at meeting; participating and voting by remote communication.

Sec. 405.

(1) A corporation may provide in its articles of incorporation or in its bylaws for a shareholder's or member's participation in a meeting of shareholders or members by a conference telephone or other means of remote communication by which all persons participating in the meeting may hear each other if all participants are advised of the means of remote communication in use and the names of the participants in the meeting are divulged to all participants.

(2) Participation in a meeting pursuant to this section constitutes presence in person at the meeting.

(3) Unless otherwise restricted by any provisions of the articles of incorporation or bylaws, the board of directors may hold a meeting of shareholders or members conducted solely by means of remote communication.

(4) Subject to any guidelines and procedures adopted by the board of directors, shareholders or members not physically present at a meeting

of shareholders or members may participate in the meeting by means of remote communication and are considered present in person and may vote at the meeting if all of the following are met:
  (a) The corporation implements reasonable measures to verify that each person considered present and permitted to vote at the meeting by means of remote communication is a shareholder or member.
  (b) The corporation implements reasonable measures to provide each shareholder or member a reasonable opportunity to participate in the meeting and to vote on matters submitted to the shareholders or members, including an opportunity to read or hear the proceedings of the meeting substantially concurrently with the proceedings.
  (c) If any shareholder or member votes or takes other action at the meeting by means of remote communication, a record of the vote or other action is maintained by the corporation.
  (d) A shareholder or member may be present and vote at an adjourned meeting of the shareholders or members by a means of remote communication if he or she was permitted to be present and vote by that means of remote communication in the original meeting notice given under section 404.

450.2406a Notice by electronic transmission.

Sec. 406a.

In addition to any other form of notice to a shareholder or member permitted by the articles of incorporation, the bylaws, or this chapter, any notice given to a shareholder or member by a form of electronic transmission to which the shareholder or member has consented is effective.

450.2407 Taking corporate action without meeting; consent; notice; statement on filed certificate; consent by electronic transmission.

Sec. 407.

(1) The articles of incorporation may provide that any action required or permitted by this act to be taken at an annual or special meeting of shareholders or members may be taken without a meeting, without prior notice, and without a vote, if consents in writing, setting forth the action taken, are signed and dated by the holders of outstanding stock or members having not less than the minimum number of votes that would

be necessary to authorize or take the action at a meeting at which all shares or members entitled to vote on the action were present and voted. Prompt notice of the taking of the corporate action without a meeting by less than unanimous written consent shall be given to shareholders or members who have not consented in writing.

(2) If an action consented to under this section would have required filing of a certificate under any other section of this act if the action had been voted upon by shareholders or members at a meeting of the shareholders or members, the certificate filed under that other section shall state, in lieu of any statement required by that section concerning a vote of shareholders or members, that both written consent and written notice have been given as provided in this section.

(3) Any action required or permitted by this act to be taken at an annual or special meeting of shareholders or members may be taken without a meeting, without prior notice, and without a vote, if all the shareholders or members entitled to vote on the action consent to the action in writing.

(4) An electronic transmission consenting to an action transmitted by a shareholder or member, or by a person authorized to act for the shareholder or member, is written, signed, and dated for the purposes of this section if the electronic transmission is delivered with information from which the corporation can determine that the electronic transmission was transmitted by the shareholder or member, or by a person authorized to act for the shareholder or member, and the date on which the electronic transmission was transmitted. The date on which an electronic transmission is transmitted is the date on which the consent was signed for purposes of this section. A consent given by electronic transmission is not delivered until reproduced in paper form and the paper form delivered to the corporation by delivery to its registered office in this state, its principal office in this state, or an officer or agent of the corporation having custody of the book in which proceedings of meetings of shareholders or members are recorded. Delivery to a corporation's registered office shall be made by hand or by certified or registered mail, return receipt requested. Delivery to a corporation's principal office in this state or to an officer or agent of the corporation having custody of the book in which proceedings of meetings of shareholders or members are recorded shall be made by hand, by certified or registered mail, return receipt requested, or in any other manner provided in the articles of incorporation or bylaws or by resolution of the board of the corporation.

450.2411 Fixing record date for determination of shareholders or members entitled to notice and vote; effect of not fixing record date; applicability of determination to adjournment.

Sec. 411.

(1) For the purpose of determining shareholders or members entitled to notice of and to vote at a meeting of shareholders or members or an adjournment thereof, or to express consent or to dissent from a proposal without a meeting, or for the purpose of any other action, the bylaws may provide for fixing, or in the absence of such provision the board may fix, in advance, a date as the record date for any such determination of shareholders or members. The date shall not be more than 60 nor less than 10 days before the date of the meeting, nor more than 60 days before any other action.

(2) If a record date is not fixed: (a) the record date for determination of shareholders or members entitled to notice of or to vote at a meeting of shareholders or members shall be the close of business on the day next preceding the day on which notice is given, or, if no notice is given, the day next preceding the day on which the meeting is held; and (b) the record date for determining shareholders or members for any purpose other than that specified in subdivision (a) shall be the close of business on the day on which the resolution of the board relating thereto is adopted.

(3) When a determination of shareholders or members of record entitled to notice of or to vote at a meeting of shareholders or members has been made as provided in this section, the determination applies to any adjournment of the meeting, unless the board fixes a new record date under this section for the adjourned meeting.

450.2413 Making and certifying list of shareholders or members entitled to vote at meeting or adjournment; requirements; noncompliance; adjournment of meeting; validity of action taken.

Sec. 413.

(1) The officer or agent having charge of the shareholder or membership records of a corporation shall make and certify a complete list of the shareholders or members entitled to vote at a shareholders' or members'

meeting or any adjourned shareholders' or members' meeting. The list shall meet all of the following:
  (a) Be arranged alphabetically within each class with the address of each member or shareholder and the number of shares held by each shareholder.
  (b) Be produced at the time and place of the meeting.
  (c) Be open to examination by any shareholder or member during the entire meeting. If the meeting is held solely by means of remote communication, then the list shall be open to the examination of any shareholder or member during the entire meeting by posting the list on a reasonably accessible electronic network, and the information required to access the list shall be provided with the notice of the meeting.
  (d) Be prima facie evidence as to who are the shareholders or members entitled to examine the list or to vote at the meeting
(2) If the requirements of this section have not been complied with, and a shareholder or member present in person or by proxy in good faith challenges the existence of sufficient votes to carry any action at the meeting, the meeting shall be adjourned until the requirements are complied with. Failure to comply with the requirements of this section does not affect the validity of an action taken at the meeting before the making of a challenge under this subsection.

450.2415 Quorum; continuing to do business notwithstanding withdrawal of shareholders or members; adjournment of meeting; shareholders entitled to vote separately.

Sec. 415.

(1) Unless a greater or lesser quorum is provided in the articles of incorporation, in a bylaw adopted by the shareholders or members, or in this act, shares or members entitled to cast a majority of the votes at a meeting constitute a quorum at the meeting. The shareholders or members present in person or by proxy at such meeting may continue to do business until adjournment, notwithstanding the withdrawal of enough shareholders or members to leave less than a quorum. Whether or not a quorum is present, the meeting may be adjourned by a vote of the shareholders or members present.
(2) When the holders of a class of shares or members of a class are entitled to vote separately on an item of business, this section applies in

determining the presence of a quorum of the class for transaction of the item of business.

450.2421 Authorizing person to act for shareholder or member by proxy; signature; duration; revocability; methods of granting authority; use of facsimile or reproduction.

Sec. 421.

(1) Except as otherwise provided in the articles of incorporation or in a bylaw adopted by the shareholders or members, a shareholder or member entitled to vote at a meeting of shareholders or members or to express consent or dissent without a meeting may authorize other persons to act for the shareholder or member by proxy.

(2) A proxy shall be signed by the shareholder or member or an authorized agent or representative. A proxy is not valid after the expiration of 3 years from its date unless otherwise provided in the proxy.

(3) A proxy is revocable at the pleasure of the shareholder or member executing it, except as otherwise provided in this section and sections 422 and 423.

(4) The authority of the holder of a proxy to act is not revoked by the incompetence or death of the shareholder or member who executed the proxy unless, before the authority is exercised, written notice of an adjudication of the incompetence or death is received by the corporate officer responsible for maintaining the list of shareholders or members.

(5) Without limiting the manner in which a shareholder or member may authorize another person or persons to act for him or her as proxy under subsection (1), each of the following methods constitute a valid means by which a shareholder or member may grant authority to another person to act as proxy:

(a) Delivering a writing to the person authorizing that person to act for the shareholder or member as proxy, executed by the shareholder or member, or by an authorized officer, director, employee, or agent of the shareholder or member, by signing the writing or causing his or her signature to be affixed to the writing by any reasonable means, including, but not limited to, facsimile signature.

(b) Transmitting or authorizing the transmission of a telegram, cablegram, or other means of electronic transmission to the person who will hold the proxy or to a proxy solicitation firm, proxy support service organization, or similar agent fully authorized by the person who will hold the proxy to receive that transmission. Any telegram, cablegram, or other means of electronic transmission must either set forth or be submitted with information from which it can be determined that the telegram, cablegram, or other electronic transmission was authorized by the shareholder or member. If a telegram, cablegram, or other electronic transmission is determined to be valid, the inspectors or, if there are no inspectors, the persons making the determination shall specify the information upon which they relied.

(c) A copy, facsimile telecommunication, or other reliable reproduction of the writing or transmission created under subsection (5) may be substituted or used in lieu of the original writing or transmission for any purpose for which the original writing or transmission could be used, if the copy, facsimile telecommunication, or other reproduction is a complete reproduction of the entire original writing or transmission.

450.2422 Irrevocable proxy.

Sec. 422.

A proxy which is entitled "irrevocable proxy", and which states that it is irrevocable, is irrevocable when it is held by any of the following or a nominee of any of the following:

(a) In the case of shares or memberships which are transferable, a pledgee.
(b) In the case of shares or memberships which are transferable, a person who has purchased or agreed to purchase the shares or members.
(c) A creditor of the corporation who extends or continues credit to the corporation in consideration of the proxy.
(d) A person who has contracted to perform services as a director, officer, or employee of the corporation, if a proxy is required by the contract of employment.
(e) A holder of any other proxy coupled with an interest.
(f) A person designated by or under an agreement under section 461.

450.2423 Revocability of proxy.

Sec. 423.

(1) A proxy becomes revocable, notwithstanding a provision making it irrevocable, after the pledge is redeemed, or the debt of the corporation is paid, or the period of employment provided for in the contract of employment has terminated, or the agreement under section 461 has terminated. In a case provided for in section 422(c) or (d) the proxy is revocable 3 years after the date of the proxy or at the end of the period, if any, specified therein, whichever period is less, unless the period of irrevocability is renewed by execution of a new irrevocable proxy. This subsection does not affect the duration of a proxy under section 421(2).

(2) A proxy is revocable, notwithstanding a provision making it irrevocable, by a purchaser of shares without knowledge of existence of the provision unless the existence of the proxy and its irrevocability are noted conspicuously on the face or back of the certificate representing the shares.

450.2431 Inspectors at shareholders' or members' meeting; waiver; appointment and duties; failure to appoint; vacancy; report; evidence.

Sec. 431.

(1) If the bylaws require inspectors at a shareholders' or members' meeting, the requirement is waived unless compliance therewith is requested by a shareholder or member present in person or by proxy and entitled to vote at the meeting. Unless otherwise provided in the bylaws, the board, in advance of a shareholders' or members' meeting, may appoint 1 or more inspectors to act at the meeting or any adjournment thereof. If inspectors are not so appointed, the person presiding at a shareholders' or members' meeting may, and on request of a shareholder or member entitled to vote shall, appoint 1 or more inspectors. In case a person appointed fails to appear or act, the vacancy may be filled by appointment made by the board in advance of the meeting or at the meeting by the person presiding.

(2) The inspectors shall determine the number of shares outstanding and the voting power of each or the members entitled to vote, the shares or members entitled to vote represented at the meeting, the existence of a quorum, the validity and effect of proxies, and shall receive votes, ballots or consents, hear and determine challenges and questions arising in connection with the right to vote, count and tabulate votes, ballots or consents, determine the result, and do such acts as are proper to conduct the election or vote with fairness to all shareholders or members. On

request of the person presiding at the meeting or a shareholder or member entitled to vote, the inspectors shall make and execute a written report to the person presiding at the meeting of any of the facts found by them and matters determined by them. The report is prima facie evidence of the facts stated and of the vote as certified by the inspectors.

450.2441 Voting generally.

Sec. 441.

(1) Each outstanding share or member is entitled to 1 vote on each matter submitted to a vote, unless otherwise provided pursuant to section 303 or 304. A vote may be cast either orally or in writing, unless otherwise provided in the bylaws. In addition, the bylaws may provide for voting by electronic transmission.

(2) When an action, other than the election of directors, is to be taken by vote of the shareholders or members, it shall be authorized by a majority of the votes cast by the holders of shares or members entitled to vote on that action, unless a greater plurality is required by the articles of incorporation or another section of this act. Except as otherwise provided by the articles, directors shall be elected by a plurality of the votes cast at an election.

450.2442 Voting as class.

Sec. 442.

(1) The articles of incorporation may provide that a class of shares or members shall vote as a class to authorize any action, including amendment to the articles. Such voting as a class shall be in addition to any other vote required by this act. Where voting as a class is provided in the articles, it shall be by the proportionate vote provided in the articles or, if a proportionate vote is not so provided, then for any action other than the election of directors, by a majority of the votes cast by the holders of shares or members of such class entitled to vote thereon.

(2) Where voting as a class is required by this act to authorize an action, the action shall be authorized by a majority of the votes cast by the holders of shares or members of each class entitled to vote thereon, unless a greater vote is required by the articles of incorporation or another section

of this act. The voting as a class shall be in addition to any other vote required by this act.

450.2443 Grouping of members in local units; basis; purpose; actions authorized by bylaws; incorporation and powers of local units; powers, rights, and privileges of elected representatives or delegates.

Sec. 443.

(1) The articles of incorporation or bylaws adopted by the members of a nonstock corporation may provide that members or a class or classes of members shall be grouped in local units, formed upon the basis of territorial units or some other reasonable basis, for the purpose of election of delegates or representatives to represent the members or the class or classes of members within such local units at any annual or special meeting or for the purpose of election of members to the board of directors.

(2) If the articles of incorporation or bylaws authorize the grouping of members in local units, the bylaws shall do, or shall authorize the board to do, the following:
   (a) Draw the local units according to the territorial limits or other reasonable basis.
   (b) Only if the grouping is for the purpose of election of delegates, determine the number of delegates to which members or each class of members within the local units are entitled, in accordance with the members' respective voting rights. Members or any class of members within each local unit who do not have voting rights shall be entitled to at least 1 delegate. Unless the articles of incorporation or bylaws otherwise provide, a delegate representing members or any class of members who do not have voting rights shall not have voting rights.
   (c) Take other actions reasonably necessary to insure the fair representation of each member within the local units at meetings of the corporation.

(3) The local units designated pursuant to this section may be incorporated under the laws of this state by the members of the local unit, and may do all things necessary to give effect to the preceding sections, the rules promulgated, and bylaws adopted under this act.

(4) Representatives or delegates elected pursuant to this section shall have and may exercise all of the powers, rights, and privileges of members at

an annual or special meeting, subject in all respects to the provisions of this act governing members.

450.2444 Voting by corporation or business corporation; voting of pledged shares.

Sec. 444.

(1) The vote of a shareholder or member which is a domestic corporation or domestic business corporation or foreign corporation or foreign business corporation, whether or not the corporation or business corporation is subject to this act, may be cast by an officer or agent, or by proxy appointed by an officer or agent or by some other person, who by action of its board or pursuant to its bylaws shall be appointed to cast such vote.
(2) A shareholder whose shares are pledged is entitled to vote the shares until they have been transferred into the name of the pledgee or a nominee of the pledgee.

450.2445 Voting of shares or membership held by person in representative or fiduciary capacity or held jointly by fiduciaries.

Sec. 445.

(1) The vote of shares or a membership held by a person in a representative or fiduciary capacity may be cast by that person without a transfer of the shares or membership into the name of the representative or fiduciary.
(2) The vote of shares or a membership held jointly by fiduciaries, where the instrument or order appointing the fiduciaries does not otherwise direct, shall be cast as follows:
 (a) If only 1 fiduciary votes, that act binds all.
 (b) If more than 1 fiduciary votes, the vote of the shares or membership shall be cast as the majority of the fiduciaries determines.
 (c) If the fiduciaries ae equally divided as to how the vote of the shares or membership shall be cast, a court having jurisdiction in an action brought by any of the fiduciaries or by any beneficiary may appoint an additional person to act with the fiduciaries in such matter, and the vote of the stock or membership shall be cast by the majority of such fiduciaries and such additional person.

450.2446 Voting of shares or membership held by joint tenants or tenants in common.

Sec. 446.

The vote of shares or a membership held by 2 or more persons as joint tenants or as tenants in common may be cast or voted at a meeting of shareholders or members by any of those persons, unless another joint tenant or tenant in common seeks to vote in person or by proxy. In the latter event, the written agreement, if any, which governs the manner in which the shares or membership shall be voted, controls if presented at the meeting, either physically or by means of electronic transmission. If the agreement is not presented at the meeting, the majority in interest of the joint tenants or tenants in common present shall control the manner of voting. In the case of a stock corporation, if there is no majority in interest of the joint tenants or tenants in common present, the shares, for the purpose of voting, shall be divided among those joint tenants or tenants in common in accordance with their interest in the shares.

450.2447 Treasury shares; shares of corporation held by another corporation or business corporation; voting.

Sec. 447.

(1) Treasury shares shall not be voted on any matter nor deemed to be outstanding shares.
(2) If a corporation holds shares sufficient to elect a majority of the directors of another domestic corporation or a foreign corporation or domestic or foreign business corporation, shares of the first corporation held by such domestic corporation or foreign corporation or domestic or foreign business corporation shall not be voted on any matter or counted in determining the total number of outstanding shares of the first corporation.

450.2448 Redemption of shares; voting.

Sec. 448.

After written notice of redemption of redeemable shares has been mailed to the holders thereof and a sum sufficient to redeem the shares has been deposited with a bank or trust company with irrevocable instruction and authority to pay the redemption price to the holders thereof upon surrender of certificates therefor, the shares shall not be voted on any matter nor deemed to be outstanding shares.

450.2451 Voting for directors.

Sec. 451.

The articles of incorporation may provide that a shareholder or member entitled to vote at an election for directors may vote, in person, by proxy, or by electronic transmission, for as many persons as there are directors to be elected and for whose election the shareholder or member has a right to vote, or to cumulate votes by giving 1 candidate as many votes as the number of those directors multiplied by the number of shares held by the shareholder or member, or by distributing the votes of the shareholder or member on the same principle among any number of the candidates.

450.2455 Action requiring vote or concurrence of greater proportion of shares, members, or class than required by act; amendment of articles.

Sec. 455.

When, with respect to an action to be taken by the shareholders or members, the articles of incorporation require the vote or concurrence of holders of a greater proportion of the shares or a greater proportion of members, or of a class thereof, than required by this act with respect to the action, the articles shall control. An amendment of the articles which adds, changes, or deletes such a provision shall be authorized by the vote required to amend the articles pursuant to section 611, or by the same vote as would be required to take action under such provision, whichever is greater.

450.2461 Agreement as to voting rights.

Sec. 461.

An agreement between 2 or more shareholders or members, if in writing and signed by the parties thereto, may provide that in exercising voting rights, they shall cast their votes as provided in the agreement, or as they may agree, or as determined in accordance with a procedure agreed upon by them.

450.2471 Shares as personal property; transfer; applicability of MCL 440.8101 to 440.8601.

Sec. 471.

The shares of a corporation are personal property. Article 8 of the uniform commercial code, 1962 PA 174, MCL 440.8101 to 440.8601, applies to the transfer of shares only to the extent not inconsistent with this act.

450.2481 Issuing or delivering unissued or treasury shares; preemptive rights.

Sec. 481.

(1) Except as otherwise provided in the articles of incorporation or by agreement, a corporation may issue or deliver unissued or treasury shares without first offering them to existing shareholders.
(2) The preemptive rights, whether created by statute or common law, of shareholders of a corporation organized before the effective date of this act are not affected by subsection (1). Such a corporation may alter or abolish its shareholders' preemptive rights by an amendment of its articles.

450.2485 Books, records, and minutes.

Sec. 485.

A corporation shall keep books and records of account and minutes of the proceedings of its shareholders or members, board, and executive committee, if any. Unless otherwise provided in the bylaws, the books, records, and minutes may be kept outside this state. The corporation shall keep at its registered office, or at the office of its transfer agent within or without this state, records containing the names and addresses of all shareholders or members, the number and class of shares held by each shareholder or the class or classes of membership held by each member and the dates when they respectively became holders of record thereof or members. Any of such books, records, or minutes may be in written form or in any other form capable of being converted into written form within a reasonable time. A corporation shall convert into written form without charge any such record not in such form, upon written request of a person entitled to inspect them.

450.2487 Mailing balance sheet and statements to shareholder or member upon request; examination of minutes and records; compelling production of books, records, and minutes; extracts.

Sec. 487.

(1) Upon written request of a shareholder or member, a corporation shall mail to the shareholder or member its balance sheet as at the end of the preceding fiscal year; its statement of income for such fiscal year; and, if prepared by the corporation, its statement of source and application of funds for such fiscal year.
(2) A person who is a shareholder or member of record of a corporation, upon at least 10 days' written demand, may examine for any proper purpose in person or by agent or attorney, during usual business hours, its minutes of shareholders' or members' meetings and record of shareholders or members and make extracts therefrom at the places where they are kept pursuant to section 485.
(3) Upon proof by a shareholder or member of a proper purpose, the circuit court may compel production for examination by the shareholder or member of the books and records of account, minutes, and record of shareholders or members of a corporation, and may allow the shareholder or member to make extracts therefrom.

450.2491 Action by shareholder or member in right of corporation to procure judgment; allegations.

Sec. 491.

(1) An action may be brought in the right of a domestic or foreign corporation to procure a judgment in its favor by a record holder or beneficial owner of shares or by a member of the corporation.
(2) In such an action, the complaint shall allege:
    (a) That the plaintiff is such a shareholder or member at the time of bringing the action and that the plaintiff was such a shareholder or member at the time of the transaction of which the plaintiff complains, or that the plaintiff's shares, interest therein, or

membership devolved upon the plaintiff by operation of law from a person who was a shareholder or member at such time.
(b) With particularity the effort of the plaintiff to secure the initiation of the action by the board or the reasons for not making the effort.

450.2492 Discontinuance, compromise, or settlement of action authorized by MCL 450.2491; approval; notice; expense; award and recovery.

Sec. 492.

An action authorized by section 491 shall not be discontinued, compromised, or settled without approval by the court having jurisdiction of the action. If the court determines that the interest of the shareholders or members or of any class thereof will be substantially affected by the discontinuance, compromise, or settlement, the court may direct that notice, by publication or otherwise, be given to the shareholders or members or any class thereof whose interests it determines will be so affected. If notice is so directed to be given, the court may determine which 1 or more of the parties to the action shall bear the expense of giving the notice, in such amount as the court determines and finds to be reasonable in the circumstances. The amount of such expense shall be awarded as special costs of the action and recoverable in the same manner as statutory taxable costs.

450.2493 Action brought in right of corporation; awarding plaintiff or claimant reasonable expenses; accounting; applicability of section; requiring plaintiff to pay expenses where action brought without reasonable cause.

Sec. 493.

(1) If an action brought in the right of the corporation is successful, in whole or in part, or if anything is received by the plaintiff or a claimant as a result of a judgment, compromise, or settlement of an action or claim, the court may award the plaintiff or claimant reasonable expenses, including reasonable attorney's fees, and shall direct the plaintiff to account to the corporation for the remainder of the proceeds received. This section does not apply to a judgment rendered for the benefit of an injured shareholder or member only and limited to a recovery of the loss or damage sustained by the injured shareholder or member.

(2) In an action brought in the right of the corporation by a record holder or beneficial owner of shares of the corporation or a member, the court having jurisdiction, upon final judgment and finding that the action was brought without reasonable cause, may require the plaintiff to pay to the parties named as defendants the reasonable expenses, including fees of attorneys, incurred by them in the defense of the action.

Chapter 5 – Management

450.2501 Management of business and affairs of corporation by board; qualifications of directors; powers of board.

Sec. 501.

(1) The business and affairs of a corporation shall be managed by its board, except as otherwise provided in this act. A director need not be a shareholder or member of the corporation unless the articles or bylaws so require. The articles or bylaws may prescribe qualifications for directors.
(2) The board of a corporation that is subject to the uniform prudent management of institutional funds act has the powers granted under both that act and this act. However, in the event of an inconsistency between the 2 acts, the uniform prudent management of institutional funds act controls.

450.2501a Board of directors; minimum age; requirements.

Sec. 501a.

(1) A corporation organized for purposes described in section 501(c)(3) of the internal revenue code of 1986 may include 1 or more directors on its board who are 16 or 17 years of age as long as that number does not exceed 1/2 the total number of directors required for a quorum for the transaction of business.
(2) If a corporation described in subsection (1) may have more than 1 director who is 16 or 17 years of age, the corporation shall state in its articles of incorporation the number of directors who may be 16 or 17 years of age.

450.2505 Board; number, term, and election or appointment of directors; resignation of director; number of directors on effective date of amendatory act.

Sec. 505.

(1) Except as provided in subsection (5), the board shall consist of 3 or more directors. The bylaws shall fix the number of directors or establish the

manner for fixing the number, unless the articles of incorporation fix the number.

(2) The articles of incorporation or a bylaw adopted by the shareholders, members, or incorporators of a corporation organized on a stock or membership basis may specify the term of office and the manner of election or appointment of directors. If the articles of incorporation or bylaws do not so specify the term of office or manner of election or appointment of directors, the first board of directors shall hold office until the first annual meeting of shareholders or members. At the first annual meeting of shareholders or members and at each subsequent annual meeting the shareholders or members shall elect directors to hold office until the succeeding annual meeting, except in case of the classification of directors permitted under this act.

(3) The articles of incorporation or a bylaw of a corporation organized on a directorship basis shall specify the term of office and the manner of election or appointment of directors.

(4) A director shall hold office for the term for which he or she is elected or appointed and until his or her successor is elected or appointed and qualified, or until his or her resignation or removal. A director may resign by written notice to the corporation. A resignation of a director is effective when it is received by the corporation or a later time if set forth in the notice of resignation.

(5) Beginning 180 days after the effective date of the amendatory act that added this subsection, the board of a corporation that is in existence on the effective date of the amendatory act that added this subsection shall consist of 3 or more directors.

450.2506 Dividing directors into 2 or more classes; election or appointment; term; expiration; election of directors by shareholders or members of class.

Sec. 506.

(1) The articles of incorporation or a bylaw adopted by the shareholders or members of a corporation organized upon a stock or membership basis may provide that in lieu of annual election of all directors the directors be divided into 2 or more classes, to be elected or appointed for such terms and in such manner as therein specified. If the articles of incorporation or the bylaws do not so specify the term of office for the classes of directors, the term of office of directors in the first class shall

expire at the first annual meeting of shareholders or members after their election, and that of each succeeding class shall expire at the next annual meeting after their election corresponding with the number of their class. At each annual meeting after such classification, a number of directors equal to the number of the class whose term expires at the time of the meeting shall be elected to hold office until the next annual meeting corresponding with the number of their class.

(2) A corporation having more than 1 class of shares or membership may provide in its articles of incorporation or a bylaw adopted by each class of shareholders or members for the election of 1 or more directors by shareholders or members of a class, to the exclusion of other shareholders or members.

(3) The articles or bylaws of a corporation organized upon a directorship basis may provide that the directors be divided into 2 or more classes, to be elected or appointed for such terms and in such manner as therein specified.

450.2511 Removal of director or entire board.

Sec. 511.

(1) Unless otherwise provided in the articles of incorporation or bylaws, a director or the entire board may be removed:
   (a) With or without cause, by vote of the holders of a majority of the shares or by majority vote of members entitled to vote at an election of directors.
   (b) With cause, by the vote of a majority of the directors then in office in the case of a corporation organized upon a directorship basis.

(2) In the case of a corporation having cumulative voting, if less than the entire board is to be removed, no 1 of the directors may be removed if the votes cast against the director's removal would be sufficient to elect the director if then cumulatively voted at an election of the entire board of directors, or, if there are classes of directors, at an election of the class of directors of which the director is a part.

(3) When shareholders or members of a class are entitled by the articles or a bylaw adopted pursuant to section 506(2) to elect 1 or more directors, this section applies, with respect to removal of a director so elected, to the vote of the holders of the outstanding shares or members of that class and not to the vote of the outstanding shares or membership as a whole.

450.2515 Filling of vacancies; increase in number of directors; special meeting where no directors in office.

Sec. 515.

(1) Unless the right to fill vacancies is reserved to the shareholders or members or otherwise provided by the articles of incorporation or bylaws, a vacancy occurring in the board may be filled by the affirmative vote of a majority of the remaining directors though less than a quorum of the board. A directorship to be filled because of an increase in the number of directors or to fill a vacancy may be filled by the board for a term of office continuing only until the next election of directors by the shareholders or members.

(2) If because of death, resignation, or other cause, a corporation has no directors in office, an officer, a shareholder, a member, an executor, administrator, trustee, or guardian of a shareholder or member, or other fiduciary entrusted with like responsibility for the person or estate of a shareholder or member, may call a special meeting of shareholders or members in accordance with the articles or the bylaws.

450.2521 Regular or special meetings of board; location; notice; waiver; participation by means of conference telephone or other remote communication.

Sec. 521.

(1) Regular or special meetings of a board may be held either in or outside of this state.
(2) A regular meeting may be held with or without notice as prescribed in the bylaws. A special meeting shall be held upon notice as prescribed in the bylaws. Attendance of a director at a meeting constitutes a waiver of notice of the meeting, except where a director attends a meeting for the express purpose of objecting to the transaction of any business because the meeting is not lawfully called or convened. Neither the business to be transacted at, nor the purpose of, a regular or special meeting need be specified in the notice or waiver of notice of the meeting unless required by the bylaws.
(3) Unless otherwise restricted by the articles of incorporation or bylaws, a member of the board or of a committee designated by the board may participate in a meeting by means of conference telephone or other

means of remote communication by which all persons participating in the meeting can communicate with each other. Participation in a meeting pursuant to this subsection constitutes presence in person at the meeting.

450.2523 Quorum; vote constituting action of board or committee; amendment of bylaws.

Sec. 523.

A majority of the members of the board then in office, or of the members of a committee thereof, constitutes a quorum for the transaction of business, provided that the articles of incorporation or bylaws may provide for a larger number, and provided further that in any corporation where there are more than 7 directors, the articles of incorporation or bylaws may provide that less than a majority, but in no event less than 1/3 of the directors, may constitute a quorum of the board. The vote of the majority of members present at a meeting at which a quorum is present constitutes the action of the board or of the committee, unless the vote of a larger number is required by this act, the articles, or the bylaws. Amendment of the bylaws by the board requires the vote of not less than a majority of the members of the board then in office.

450.2525 Taking action without meeting; consent.

Sec. 525.

Unless prohibited by the articles of incorporation or bylaws, action required or permitted to be taken under authorization voted at a meeting of the board or a committee of the board may be taken without a meeting if, before or after the action, all members of the board then in office or of the committee consent to the action in writing or by electronic transmission. The written consents shall be filed with the minutes of the proceedings of the board or committee. The consent has the same effect as a vote of the board or committee for all purposes.

450.2527 Designation of committees; membership; alternates; term; providing for election or appointment of committees in articles or bylaws.

Sec. 527.

(1) Unless otherwise provided in the articles of incorporation or bylaws, the board may designate 1 or more committees, each committee to consist of 1 or more of the directors of the corporation. The board may designate 1 or more directors as alternate members of a committee, who may replace an absent or disqualified member at a meeting of the committee. The bylaws may provide that in the absence or disqualification of a member of a committee, the members thereof present at a meeting and not disqualified from voting, whether or not they constitute a quorum, may unanimously appoint another member of the board to act at the meeting in place of such an absent or disqualified member.
(2) A committee designated pursuant to subsection (1), and each member thereof, shall serve at the pleasure of the board.
(3) The articles of incorporation or bylaws may provide for the election or appointment of 1 or more committees to consist of 1 or more shareholders or members or 1 or more directors or a combination of shareholders or members and directors.

450.2528 Committee designated pursuant to MCL 450.2527; powers and authority.

Sec. 528.

A committee designated pursuant to section 527, to the extent provided in the resolution of the board in the case of a committee designated in section 527(1), or to the extent provided in the articles or in the bylaws in the case of a committee designated in section 527(3), may exercise any or all powers and authority of the board in management of the business and affairs of the corporation. However, such a committee does not have power or authority to:
(a) Amend the articles of incorporation.
(b) Adopt an agreement of merger or consolidation.
(c) Recommend to shareholders or members the sale, lease, or exchange of all or substantially all of the corporation's property and assets.
(d) Recommend to shareholders or members a dissolution of the corporation or a revocation of a dissolution.
(e) Amend the bylaws of the corporation.
(f) Fill vacancies in the board.
(g) Fix compensation of the directors for serving on the board or on a committee.
(h) Cancel stock or terminate membership.

450.2531 Officers of corporation; election or appointment; person holding 2 or more offices; term of office; authority and duties.

Sec. 531.

(1) The officers of a corporation shall consist of a president, secretary, treasurer, and, if desired, a chairperson of the board, 1 or more vicepresidents, and such other officers as may be prescribed by the bylaws or determined by the board. Unless otherwise provided in the articles of incorporation or bylaws, the officer shall be elected or appointed by the board.

(2) Two or more offices may be held by the same person, but an officer shall not execute, acknowledge, or verify an instrument in more than 1 capacity if the instrument is required by law or the articles or bylaws to be executed, acknowledged, or verified by 2 or more officers.

(3) An officer elected or appointed as herein provided shall hold office for the term for which the officer is elected or appointed and until a successor is elected or appointed and qualified, or until the resignation or removal of the officer.

(4) An officer, as between that officer, other officers, and the corporation, has such authority and shall perform such duties in the management of the corporation as may be provided in the bylaws, or as may be determined by resolution of the board not inconsistent with the bylaws.

450.2535 Removal of officer; suspension of authority to act; contract rights; resignation of officer; notice.

Sec. 535.

(1) An officer elected or appointed by the board may be removed by the board with or without cause. An officer elected by the shareholders or members may be removed, with or without cause, only by vote of the shareholders or members. The authority of the officer to act as an officer may be suspended by the board for cause.

(2) The removal of an officer shall be without prejudice to the contract rights of the officer, if any. The election or appointment of an officer does not of itself create contract rights.

(3) An officer may resign by written notice to the corporation. The resignation is effective upon its receipt by the corporation or at a subsequent time specified in the notice of resignation.

450.2541 Director or officer; discharge of duties; compliance; liability of volunteer director; action against director or officer for failure to perform duties.

Sec. 541.

(1) A director or an officer shall discharge the duties of that position in good faith and with the degree of diligence, care, and skill that an ordinarily prudent person would exercise under similar circumstances in a like position. In discharging the duties, a director or an officer, when acting in good faith, may rely upon the opinion of counsel for the corporation, upon the report of an independent appraiser selected with reasonable care by the board, or upon financial statements of the corporation represented to the director or officer as correct by the president or the officer of the corporation who has charge of its books or account, or as stated in a written report by an independent public or certified public accountant or firm of accountants fairly to reflect the financial condition of the corporation.

(2) A director or officer of a corporation subject to the uniform prudent management of institutional funds act, shall be considered to be in compliance with this section if the director or officer complies with the uniform prudent management of institutional funds act in the administration of the powers specified in that act.

(3) If the corporation's articles of incorporation contain a provision authorized under section 209(c), a volunteer director of the corporation is only personally liable for monetary damages for a breach of fiduciary duty as a director to the corporation, its shareholders, or its members to the extent set forth in the provision.

(4) If the corporation's articles of incorporation contain a provision authorized under section 209(d), a claim for monetary damages for a breach of a volunteer director's duty to any person other than the corporation, its shareholders, or its members shall not be brought or maintained against the volunteer director. The claim shall be brought or maintained instead against the corporation, which shall be liable for any breach of the volunteer director's duty.

(5) An action against a director or officer for failure to perform the duties imposed by this section shall be commenced within 3 years after the cause of action has accrued, or within 2 years after the time when the

cause of action is discovered, or should reasonably have been discovered, by the complainant, whichever occurs first.

450.2545 Transaction between corporation and directors or officers, or between corporation and corporation or business corporation, firm, or association in which directors or officers interested, not void or voidable; conditions.

Sec. 545.

A contract or other transaction between a corporation and 1 or more of its directors or officers, or between a corporation and a domestic or foreign corporation, domestic or foreign business corporation, firm, or association of any type or kind, in which 1 or more of its directors or officers are directors or officers, or are otherwise interested, is not void or voidable solely because of such common directorship, officership, or interest, or solely because such directors are present at the meeting of the board or committee thereof which authorizes or approves the contract or transaction, or solely because their votes are counted for such purpose if any of the following conditions is satisfied:
(a) The contract or other transaction is fair and reasonable to the corporation when it is authorized, approved, or ratified.
(b) The material facts as to the director's or officer's relationship or interest and as to the contract or transaction are disclosed or known to the board or committee, and the board or committee authorizes, approves, or ratifies the contract or transaction by a vote sufficient for the purpose without counting the vote of any common or interested director.
(c) The material facts as to the director's or officer's relationship or interest and as to the contract or transaction are disclosed or known to the shareholders or members, and they authorize, approve or ratify the contract or transaction.

450.2546 Burden of establishing validity of contract described in MCL 450.2545; grounds; counting common or interested directors in determining presence of quorum; compensation of directors; approval of shareholders or members.

Sec. 546.

(1) When the validity of a contract described in section 545 is questioned, the burden of establishing its validity on the grounds prescribed in

section 545 is upon the director, officer, corporation, firm, or association asserting its validity.

(2) Common or interested directors may be counted in determining the presence of a quorum at a board or committee meeting at which a contract or transaction described in section 545 is authorized, approved, or ratified.

(3) The board, by affirmative vote of a majority of directors in office and irrespective of any personal interest of any of them, may establish reasonable compensation of directors for services to the corporation as directors or officers, but approval of the shareholders or members is required if the articles of incorporation, bylaws, or other provisions of this act so provide.

450.2548 Loan, guaranty, or assistance by corporation for officer or employee; corporation as charitable purpose corporation.

Sec. 548.

(1) Except as provided in subsection (4) and unless otherwise prohibited by law, a corporation may lend money to, or guarantee an obligation of, or otherwise assist an officer or employee of the corporation or a subsidiary, including an officer or employee who is a director of the corporation or subsidiary, if in the judgment of the board, the loan, guaranty, or assistance is reasonably expected to benefit the corporation.

(2) A loan, guaranty, or assistance described in subsection (1) may be with or without interest, and may be unsecured, or secured in a manner that the board approves.

(3) This section does not deny, limit, or restrict the powers of guaranty or warranty of a corporation at common law or under any statute.

(4) If a corporation is a charitable purpose corporation, the corporation shall not provide loans to or guarantee an obligation of an officer or director of the corporation or a subsidiary of a corporation, unless the officer or director is also a client of the corporation and the loan or guaranty is necessary to carry out the corporation's charitable purposes.

450.2551 Liability of directors for certain corporate actions; liability of shareholder or member accepting or receiving unauthorized distribution.

Sec. 551.

(1) In addition to any other liability imposed by this act or other law upon directors of a corporation, directors who vote for, or concur in, any of the following corporate actions are jointly and severally liable to the corporation for the benefit of its creditors, shareholders, or members, to the extent of any legally recoverable injury suffered by such persons as a result of the action but not to exceed the amount unlawfully paid or distributed:
  (a) Distribution of assets to shareholders or members contrary to this act or contrary to any restriction in the articles of incorporation or bylaws.
  (b) Purchase of shares or memberships of the corporation contrary to this act or contrary to any restriction in the articles or bylaws.
  (c) Distribution of assets to shareholders or members during or after dissolution of the corporation without paying, or adequately providing for, all known debts, obligations, and liabilities of the corporation.
  (d) Making of a loan to an officer, director, or employee of the corporation or of a subsidiary thereof contrary to this act.
(2) A director is not liable under this section if the director has complied with section 541.
(3) A shareholder or member who accepts or receives a distribution with knowledge of facts indicating it is not authorized by this act is liable to the corporation in the amount accepted or received by the shareholder or member.

450.2552 Rights of director against whom claim successfully asserted under MCL 450.2551.

Sec. 552.

(1) A director against whom a claim is successfully asserted under section 551 is entitled to contribution from the other directors who voted for, or concurred in, the action upon which the claim is asserted.
(2) A director against whom a claim is successfully asserted under section 551 is entitled, to the extent of the amounts paid by the director to the corporation as a result of such claims:
  (a) Upon payment to the corporation of any amount of an improper distribution, to be subrogated to the rights of the corporation against shareholders or members who received the distribution in proportion to the amounts received by them respectively.

(b) Upon payment to the corporation of any amount of the purchase price of an improper purchase of shares or memberships: (i) to have the corporation rescind the purchase and recover for the director's benefit, but at the director's expense, the amount of the purchase price from any seller who sold such shares or memberships with knowledge of facts indicating that such purchase of shares or memberships by the corporation was not authorized by this act; or (ii) to have the corporation assign to such director any claim against the seller and, if consistent with its articles of incorporation and bylaws, such shares or memberships.

(c) Upon payment to the corporation of the claim of a creditor because of a violation of section 551(1)(c), to be subrogated to the rights of the corporation against shareholders or members who received an improper distribution of assets.

(d) Upon payment to the corporation of the amount of a loan made improperly to an officer, director, or employee, to be subrogated to the rights of the corporation against an officer, director, or employee who received the improper loan.

450.2553 Presence or absence of director at meeting at which action referred to in MCL 450.2551 taken; presumption; dissent.

Sec. 553.

A director who is present at a meeting of the board, or a committee thereof of which the director is a member, at which action on a corporate matter referred to in section 551 is taken, is presumed to have concurred in that action unless a dissent is entered in the minutes of the meeting or unless the director files a written dissent to the action with the person acting as secretary of the meeting before or promptly after the adjournment thereof. The right to dissent does not apply to a director who voted in favor of the action. A director who is absent from a meeting of the board, or a committee thereof of which the director is a member, at which any such action is taken is presumed to have concurred in the action unless the director files a dissent with the secretary of the corporation within a reasonable time after obtaining knowledge of the action.

450.2554 Commencement of action under MCL 450.2551 or 450.2552.

Sec. 554.

An action against a director, shareholder, or member for recovery upon a liability imposed by section 551 shall be commenced within 3 years after the cause of action accrues. An action under section 552 shall be commenced within 3 years after payment by the director to the corporation.

450.2556 Volunteer's acts or omissions; claim for monetary damages.

Sec. 556.

If the corporation's articles of incorporation contain a provision authorized under section 209(e), then a claim for monetary damages for a volunteer director, volunteer officer, or other volunteer's acts or omissions shall not be brought or maintained against a volunteer director, volunteer officer, or other volunteer. The claim shall be brought and maintained against the corporation.

450.2561 Indemnification of director, officer, partner, trustee, employee, nondirector volunteer, or agent in connection with action, suit, or proceeding; conditions; presumption.

Sec. 561.

Unless otherwise provided by law or its articles of incorporation or bylaws, a corporation has the power to indemnify a person who was or is a party or is threatened to be made a party to any threatened, pending, or completed action, suit, or proceeding, whether civil, criminal, administrative, or investigative and whether formal or informal, other than an action by or in the right of the corporation, by reason of the fact that the person is or was a director, officer, employee, nondirector volunteer, or agent of the corporation, or is or was serving at the request of the corporation as a director, officer, partner, trustee, employee, nondirector volunteer, or agent of another foreign or domestic corporation, business corporation, partnership, joint venture, trust, or other enterprise, whether for profit or not for profit, against expenses including attorneys' fees, judgments, penalties, fines, and amounts paid in settlement actually and reasonably incurred by the person in connection with the action, suit, or proceeding if the person acted in good faith and in a manner the person reasonably believed to be in or not opposed to the best interests of the corporation or its shareholders or members, and with respect to any criminal action or proceeding, if the person had no reasonable cause to believe that conduct was unlawful. The termination of any action, suit, or proceeding by judgment, order, settlement, conviction, or upon a plea of nolo contendere or its equivalent shall not of itself create a presumption that the person did not act in good faith and in a manner which the person reasonably believed to be in or not opposed to the best interests of the corporation or its shareholders or members and, with respect to any criminal action or proceeding, had reasonable cause to believe that the conduct was unlawful.

450.2562 Indemnification against expenses of director, officer, partner, trustee, employee, nondirector volunteer, or agent in connection with action or suit by or in right of corporation; conditions; limitations.

Sec. 562.

Unless otherwise provided by law or its articles of incorporation or bylaws, a corporation has the power to indemnify a person who was or is a party to or is threatened to be made a party to a threatened, pending, or completed action or suit by or in the right of the corporation to procure a judgment in its favor by reason of the fact that the person is or was a director, officer, employee, nondirector volunteer, or agent of the corporation, or is or was serving at the request of the corporation as a director, officer, partner, trustee, employee, nondirector volunteer, or agent of another foreign or domestic corporation, business corporation, partnership, joint venture, trust, or other enterprise whether for profit or not against expenses, including actual and reasonable attorneys' fees, and amounts paid in settlement incurred by the person in connection with the action or suit if the person acted in good faith and in a manner the person reasonably believed to be in or not opposed to the best interests of the corporation or its shareholders or members. However, indemnification shall not be made for a claim, issue, or matter in which the person has been found liable to the corporation unless and only to the extent that the court in which the action or suit was brought has determined upon application that, despite the adjudication of liability but in view of all circumstances of the case, the person is fairly and reasonably entitled to indemnification for expenses which the court considers proper.

450.2563 Indemnification against expenses of director, officer, employee, nondirector volunteer, or agent successful in defense of action, suit, or proceeding referred to in MCL 450.2561 or 450.2562; authorization; determination; indemnification for portion of expenses.

Sec. 563.

(1) Unless otherwise provided by law or its articles of incorporation or bylaws, to the extent that a director, officer, employee, nondirector volunteer, or agent of a corporation has been successful on the merits or otherwise in defense of an action, suit, or proceeding referred to in section 561 or 562, or in defense of a claim, issue, or matter in the action, suit, or proceeding, the successful party shall be indemnified against expenses, including actual and reasonable attorneys' fees, incurred in connection with the action, suit, or proceeding and in any action, suit, or proceeding brought to enforce the mandatory indemnification provided in this subsection.

(2) An indemnification under section 561 or 562, unless ordered by a court, shall be made by the corporation only as authorized in the specific case upon a determination that indemnification of the director, officer, employee, nondirector volunteer, or agent is proper in the circumstances because the person has met the applicable standard of conduct set forth in sections 561 and 562. This determination shall be made in any of the following ways:
   (a) By a majority vote of a quorum of the board consisting of directors who were not parties to the action, suit, or proceeding.
   (b) If the quorum described in subdivision (a) is not obtainable, then by a majority vote of a committee of directors who are not parties to the action. The committee shall consist of not less than 2 disinterested directors.
   (c) By independent legal counsel in a written opinion.
   (d) By the shareholders or members.

(3) If a person is entitled to indemnification under section 561 or 562 for a portion of expenses including attorneys' fees, judgments, penalties, fines, and amounts paid in settlement but not for the total amount thereof, the corporation may indemnify the person for the portion of the expenses, judgments, penalties, fines, or amounts paid in settlement for which the person is entitled to be indemnified.

450.2564 Advance payment by corporation of expenses incurred in defending action, suit, or proceeding described in MCL 450.2561 or 450.2562; repayment.

Sec. 564.

Expenses incurred in defending a civil or criminal action, suit, or proceeding described in section 561 or 562 may be paid by the corporation in advance of the final disposition of the action, suit, or proceeding upon receipt of an undertaking by or on behalf of the director, officer, employee, nondirector volunteer, or agent to repay the expenses if it is ultimately determined that the person is not entitled to be indemnified by the corporation. The undertaking shall be by unlimited general obligation of the person on whose behalf advances are made but need not be secured.

450.2565 Indemnification or advancement of expenses not exclusive of other rights; limitation; continuation of indemnification.

Sec. 565.

(1) The indemnification or advancement of expenses provided under sections 561 to 564 is not exclusive of other rights to which a person seeking indemnification or advancement of expenses may be entitled under the articles of incorporation, bylaws, or a contractual agreement. However, the total amount of expenses advanced or indemnified from all sources combined shall not exceed the amount of actual expenses incurred by the person seeking indemnification or advancement of expenses.

(2) The indemnification provided in sections 561 to 564 and this section continues as to a person who ceases to be a director, officer, employee, nondirector volunteer, or agent and shall inure to the benefit of the heirs, executors, and administrators of the person.

450.2567 Purchase and maintenance of insurance on behalf of director, officer, employee, nondirector volunteer, or agent.

Sec. 567.

A corporation shall have power to purchase and maintain insurance on behalf of any person who is or was a director, officer, employee, nondirector volunteer, or agent of the corporation, or is or was serving at the request of the corporation as a director, officer, employee, nondirector volunteer, or agent of another corporation, business corporation, partnership, joint venture, trust, or other enterprise against any liability asserted against the person and incurred by the person in any such capacity or arising out of the person's status as such, whether or not the corporation would have power to indemnify the person against such liability under sections 561 to 565.

450.2569 Scope of "corporation" for purposes of MCL 450.2561 to 450.2567; effect.

Sec. 569.

For purposes of sections 561 to 567, "corporation" includes all constituent corporations absorbed in a consolidation or merger and the resulting or surviving corporation or business corporation, so that a person who is or was a director, officer, employee, nondirector volunteer, or agent of the constituent corporation or is or was serving at the request of the constituent corporation as a director, officer, partner, trustee, employee, nondirector volunteer, or agent of another foreign or domestic corporation, business corporation, partnership, joint venture, trust, or other enterprise whether for profit or not shall stand in the same position under the provisions of this section with respect to the resulting or surviving corporation or business corporation as the person would if the person had served the resulting or surviving corporation or business corporation in the same capacity.

Chapter 6 – Amending Corporate Documents

450.2601 Amendment of articles of incorporation; contents.

Sec. 601.

(1) A corporation may amend its articles of incorporation if the amendment contains only such provisions as might lawfully be contained in original articles of incorporation filed at the time of making the amendment.
(2) Subject to section 301(5), a corporation may amend its articles of incorporation to become a business corporation by adopting restated articles of incorporation in accordance with section 641 which shall so amend the articles that they shall contain only such provisions as might be lawfully contained in original articles of incorporation of a business corporation organized under Act No. 284 of the Public Acts of 1972, as amended, being sections 450.1101 to 450.2099 of the Michigan Compiled Laws.

450.2602 Amendment of articles of incorporation; purposes.

Sec. 602.

Without limitation upon the general power of amendment granted by section 601, a corporation may amend its articles of incorporation:
(a) To change its corporate name.
(b) To enlarge, limit, or otherwise change its corporate purposes or powers.
(c) To change the duration of the corporation.
(d) To increase or decrease the aggregate number of shares, or shares of any class which the corporation has authority to issue.
(e) To exchange, classify, reclassify, or cancel any of its issued or unissued shares.
(f) To change the designation of any of its issued or unissued shares, and to change the qualifications, preferences, limitations, and relative rights in respect of any of its issued or unissued shares or of its members.
(g) To change the issued or unissued shares of any class into a different number of shares of the same class or into the same or a different number of shares of other classes.
(h) To create new classes of shares or members having rights and preferences superior or inferior to, or equal with the issued or unissued shares or the members of any class then authorized.

(i) To change its registered office or change its resident agent.
(j) To strike out, change, or add any provision for management of the business and conduct of the affairs of the corporation, or creating, defining, limiting, and regulating the powers of the corporation, its director and shareholders or members or any class of shareholders or members, including any provision which under this act is required or permitted to be set forth in the bylaws.
(k) To change its basis of organization to a stock corporation or a nonstock corporation organized upon a membership or directorship basis, in which event the amendment shall comply with section 202(c) and (d) or section 202(e) and (f), as applicable.

450.2611 Amendment of articles by incorporators; manner of adoption; notice of meeting; vote on proposed amendment; requirements; adoption; number of amendments acted upon at 1 meeting; certificate of amendment.

Sec. 611.

(1) Before the first meeting of the board, the incorporators may amend the articles of incorporation by complying with section 631(1).
(2) Except for an amendment described in subsection (1) and except as otherwise provided in this act, a corporation must adopt any amendment to the articles of incorporation in 1 of the following manners as provided in this section:
　(a) If the corporation is organized on a membership basis, by a vote of the members entitled to vote on the amendment.
　(b) If the corporation is organized on a stock basis, by a vote of the shareholders entitled to vote on the amendment.
　(c) If the corporation is organized on a directorship basis, unless the articles of incorporation specify a different manner, by a vote of the directors.
(3) A corporation shall give notice of a meeting to consider an amendment to the articles of incorporation to each member, shareholder, or director entitled to vote on the amendment, as applicable. The notice shall contain the proposed amendment or a summary of the changes that will occur if the amendment is adopted. The corporation shall provide the notice within the time and in the manner provided in this act for giving notice of meetings of shareholders, members, or directors, except that the

corporation shall give notice of the meeting to each director then in office not less than 10 days before the meeting.

(4) At a meeting to consider an amendment to the articles of incorporation, a vote of shareholders, members, or directors entitled to vote shall be taken on the proposed amendment. The proposed amendment is adopted if it receives the affirmative vote of a majority of the outstanding shares or members entitled to vote on the proposed amendment or a majority of the directors then in office. If any class of shares or members is entitled to vote on the proposed amendment as a class, the affirmative vote of a majority of the outstanding shares or members of that class is also required to adopt the amendment. The voting requirements of this section are subject to greater requirements as prescribed by this act for specific amendments, or as provided in the articles of incorporation or bylaws. In addition, unless a greater vote is required in the articles of incorporation, or in a bylaw adopted by the shareholders, members, or directors, the proposed amendment is adopted if it receives an affirmative vote of a majority of members or shares of shareholders present in person, by proxy, or by electronic transmission at the meeting if due notice of the time, place, and object of the meeting was given by mail, at the last known address, to each shareholder, member, or director entitled to vote at least 20 days before the date of the meeting or by publication in a publication distributed by the corporation to its shareholders or members at least 20 days before the date of the meeting.

(5) The shareholders, members, or directors may act on any number of amendments at 1 meeting.

(6) If an amendment to the articles of incorporation is adopted, the corporation shall file a certificate of amendment as provided in section 631.

450.2615 Voting as class upon proposed amendment.

Sec. 615.

The holders of the outstanding shares or the member of a class may vote as a class upon a proposed amendment, whether or not entitled to vote thereon by the articles of incorporation, if the amendment would increase or decrease the aggregate number of authorized shares of the class or alter or change the powers, preferences, or special rights of the shares or members of the class or other classes so as to affect the class adversely.

450.2631 Certificate of amendment; signing or execution; filing; contents.

Sec. 631.

(1) If the amendment is made as provided in section 611(1), a certificate of amendment shall be signed by all the incorporators and filed on behalf of the corporation, setting forth the amendment and certifying that the amendment is adopted by unanimous consent of the incorporators before the first meeting of the board.
(2) In case of any other amendment, except as otherwise provided in this act, a certificate of amendment shall be executed and filed on behalf of the corporation setting forth the amendment and certifying that the amendment has been adopted in accordance with section 611(2).

450.2641 Integrating provisions of articles into single instrument; adoption of restated articles of incorporation; amendments subject to other provisions of act.

Sec. 641.

(1) A corporation may integrate into a single instrument the provisions of its articles of incorporation which are then in effect and operative, as theretofore amended, and at the same time may also further amend its articles of incorporation by adopting restated articles of incorporation.
(2) If the restated articles of incorporation merely restate and integrate, but do not further amend the articles as theretofore amended, they may be adopted by the board without a vote of the shareholders or members, or by the shareholders or members, in which case the procedure and vote required by section 611(2) is applicable. If the restated articles of incorporation restate and integrate and also further amend in any material respect the articles of incorporation, as theretofore amended, they shall be adopted by the shareholders, members, or directors pursuant to section 611(2).
(3) An amendment effected in connection with the reinstatement and integration of the articles of incorporation is subject to any other provision of this act, not inconsistent with this section, which would apply if a certificate of amendment were filed to effect such amendment.

450.2642 Restated articles of incorporation; designation; required statements; omitted provisions.

Sec. 642.

Restated articles of incorporation shall be specifically designated as such in the heading thereof. They shall state, either in the heading or in an introductory paragraph, the corporation's present name, and, if it has been changed, all of its former names and the date of filing of its original articles. Restated articles shall state that they were duly adopted by directors, shareholders, or members in accordance with this section. If adopted by the board without a vote of the shareholders, members, or directors according to the procedure and vote required by section 641(2), they shall state that they only restate and integrate and do not further amend the articles as theretofore amended, and that there is no material discrepancy between those provisions and the provisions of the restated articles. Restated articles of incorporation may omit such provisions of the original articles which named the incorporators, the initial board, or original subscribers for shares or original members, and the omission is not deemed a further amendment.

450.2643 Restated articles of incorporation; execution; filing; effect.

Sec. 643.

Restated articles of incorporation shall be executed and filed in accordance with section 131. When such filing becomes effective, the corporation's original articles of incorporation, as amended, are superseded; and thenceforth the restated articles, including any further amendments made thereby, shall be the articles of incorporation of the corporation.

450.2651 Abandonment of amendment; certificate.

Sec. 651.

Before the effective date of an amendment to the articles of incorporation for which shareholder, member, or director approval is required by this act, the amendment may be abandoned pursuant to provisions therefor, if any, set forth in the resolution of the shareholders, members, or directors approving the amendment. If a certificate of amendment has been filed by the corporation, it shall file a certificate of abandonment, but not later than the proposed effective date within 10 days after the abandonment.

Chapter 7 – Merger and Consolidation

450.2701 Merger or consolidation of domestic corporations; plan; contents.

Sec. 701.

(1) Two or more domestic corporations may merge into 1 of the corporations or consolidate into a new corporation pursuant to a plan of merger or consolidation approved in the manner provided in this act.
(2) The board of each corporation proposing to participate in a merger or consolidation shall adopt a plan of merger or consolidation, setting forth:
    (a) The name of each constituent corporation and the name of the surviving or consolidated corporation.
    (b) As to each constituent corporation which is a stock corporation, the designation and number of outstanding shares of each class, specifying the classes entitled to vote; and each class, if any, entitled to vote as a class; and, if the number of any such shares is subject to change before the effective date of the merger or consolidation, the manner in which the change may occur.
    (c) As to each constituent corporation which is a nonstock corporation, a description of the members, in the case of a membership corporation, including the number, classification, and voting rights of members, or a description of the organization of the board, in the case of a directorship corporation, including the number, classification, and voting rights of directors.
    (d) The terms and conditions of the proposed merger or consolidation, including the manner and basis of converting the shares of or membership or other interest in each constituent corporation into shares, bonds, or other securities or membership or other interest in the surviving or consolidated corporation, or into cash or other consideration, which may include shares, bonds, rights, or other property or securities of a corporation whether or not a party to the merger, or into a combination thereof.
    (e) In a merger, a statement of an amendment to the articles of incorporation of the surviving corporation to be effected by the merger or a restatement of the articles of incorporation as provided in section 641(1), which shall be in the form of restated articles of incorporation as provided in section 642; and in a consolidation, all

statements required to be included in articles of incorporation formed under this act.

(f) Other provisions with respect to the proposed merger or consolidation as the board considers necessary or desirable.

450.2703 Plan of merger or consolidation; approval or authorization; voting; notice of meeting.

Sec. 703.

(1) A plan of merger or consolidation adopted by the board of each constituent corporation which is organized upon a stock or membership basis shall be submitted for approval at a meeting of its shareholders or members. Notice of the meeting shall be given to each shareholder or member of record, whether or not entitled to vote at the meeting, not less than 20 days before the meeting, in the manner provided in this act for the giving of notice of meetings of shareholders or members. The notice shall include or be accompanied by a copy or summary of the plan of merger or consolidation.

(2) At the meeting, a vote of the shareholders or members shall be taken on the proposed plan of merger or consolidation. The plan shall be approved upon receiving the affirmative vote of a majority of the outstanding shares or members of the corporation entitled to vote thereon, and if a class is entitled to vote thereon as a class, the affirmative vote of a majority of the outstanding shares or members of each such class. A class of shares or members of any such corporation is entitled to vote as a class if the plan of merger or consolidation contains a provision which, if contained in a proposed amendment to the articles of incorporation, would entitle the class of shares or members to vote as a class.

(3) If any merging or consolidating corporation is organized upon a directorship basis, a plan of merger or consolidation shall be authorized upon receiving the affirmative vote of a majority of the directors then in office. Notice of the meeting to authorize the plan of merger or consolidation shall be given to each director then in office not less than 20 days before the meeting and shall include or be accompanied by a copy or summary of the plan.

450.2707 Certificate of merger or certificate of consolidation; execution and filing; contents; effective date.

Sec. 707.

(1) After approval of a plan of merger or consolidation, a certificate of merger or a certificate of consolidation shall be executed and filed on behalf of each corporation. The certificate shall set forth the plan of merger or the plan of consolidation and either of the following:
   (a) A statement that the plan of merger or consolidation has been adopted by the board and approved by the shareholders or members in accordance with sections 701 to 703(1) and (2).
   (b) A statement that the plan of merger or consolidation has been adopted by the board in accordance with section 703(3).
(2) The certificate of merger or consolidation shall become effective in accordance with section 131.

450.2721 Effect of merger or consolidation.

Sec. 721.

When a merger or consolidation has been effected:
(a) The corporations parties to the plan of merger or consolidation shall be a single corporation, which in a merger is that corporation designated in the plan of merger as the surviving corporation, and in a consolidation is the new corporation provided for in the plan of consolidation.
(b) The separate existence of corporations parties to the plan of merger or consolidation, except the surviving or new corporation, shall cease.
(c) The surviving or new corporation has all the rights, privileges, immunities, and powers and is subject to all the duties and liabilities of a corporation organized under this act.

450.2722 Surviving or new corporation; rights, privileges, immunities, and franchises; liabilities and obligations; prosecution of existing claim or pending action or proceeding; rights of creditors; lien upon property of corporation.

Sec. 722.

(1) The surviving or new corporation has all the rights, privileges, immunities, and franchises, public or private, of each of the merging or consolidating corporations; and all property, real, personal, and mixed, and all debts due on whatever account, including subscriptions to shares,

and all other choses in action. Upon complying with section 217, the surviving or new corporation may use the corporate name and the assumed names of the merging or consolidating corporations. All interests of or belonging to or due to each of the corporations merged or consolidated, are considered to be transferred to and vested in a single corporation without further act or deed. The title to real estate, or any interest in real estate, vested in a corporation shall not revert or be in any way impaired because of the merger or consolidation.

(2) The surviving or new corporation is thenceforth responsible and liable for all liabilities and obligations of each of the corporations merged or consolidated. A claim existing or action or proceeding pending by or against a corporation may be prosecuted as if the merger or consolidation had not taken place, or the surviving or new corporation may be substituted in its place. The rights of creditors and a lien upon the property of such a corporation are not impaired by the merger or consolidation.

450.2723 Changes in articles stated in plan of merger; effect; statements in plan of consolidation as original articles of new corporation.

Sec. 723.

In a merger, the articles of incorporation of the surviving corporation are deemed to be amended to the extent, if any, that changes in its articles are stated in the plan of merger. In a consolidation, the statements set forth in the plan of consolidation and which are required or permitted to be set forth in the articles of incorporation of a corporation organized under this act are deemed to be the original articles of the new corporation.

450.2731 Merger or consolidation of foreign and domestic corporations; compliance with laws of jurisdiction; applicability of act to surviving or new corporation governed by laws of other jurisdiction; liability of corporation; service of process.

Sec. 731.

(1) One or more foreign corporations and 1 or more domestic corporations may be merged or consolidated as provided in this act, if the merger or consolidation is permitted by the laws of the jurisdiction where each foreign corporation is organized.

(2) A domestic corporation shall comply with this act with respect to the merger or consolidation of domestic corporations and a foreign corporation shall comply with the laws of the jurisdiction where it is organized.

(3) If the surviving or new corporation is to be governed by the laws of a jurisdiction other than this state, it shall comply with the provisions of this act with respect to foreign corporations if it is to conduct affairs in this state. The corporation is liable, and is subject to service of process of a proceeding in this state, for the enforcement of an obligation of a domestic corporation which is a party to the merger or consolidation.

450.2732 Effect of merger or consolidation authorized by MCL 450.2731.

Sec. 732.

The effect of a merger or consolidation authorized by section 731 is the same as in the case of a merger or consolidation of domestic corporations, if the surviving or new corporation is to be governed by the laws of this state. If the surviving or new corporation is to be governed by the laws of a jurisdiction other than this state, the effect of the merger or consolidation is the same as in the case of the merger or consolidation in such jurisdiction, except as otherwise herein provided.

450.2736 Merger or consolidation of domestic corporations and domestic or foreign business corporations; procedure; compliance with applicable laws; plan of merger or consolidation; applicability of act to surviving or new corporation or business corporation governed by laws of other jurisdiction; liability of corporation or business corporation; service of process.

Sec. 736.

(1) Subject to section 301(5), one or more domestic corporations and 1 or more domestic business corporations and foreign business corporations may be merged or consolidated as provided in this act, if such merger or consolidation is not contrary to the law of the state of incorporation of any constituent foreign business corporation.

(2) With respect to procedure, including authorization by shareholders, members, or directors, each domestic corporation shall comply with the provisions of this act, each domestic business corporation shall comply

with the provisions of Act No. 284 of the Public Acts of 1972, as amended, being sections 450.1101 to 450.2099 of the Michigan Compiled Laws, and each foreign business corporation shall comply with the applicable provisions of the law of the jurisdiction where it is organized.

(3) The plan of merger or consolidation shall set forth, in addition to all matters required by section 701(2), the manner and basis of converting shares, membership or other interests in each constituent corporation or business corporation into shares, membership, or other interests of the surviving or consolidated corporation or business corporation, or the case or other consideration to be paid or delivered in exchange for shares, membership, or other interests in each constituent corporation or business corporation, or a combination thereof.

(4) If the surviving or new corporation or business corporation is to be governed by the laws of a jurisdiction other than this state, it shall comply with the provisions of this act with respect to foreign corporations or foreign business corporations if it is to conduct affairs or to transact business in this state. The corporation or business corporation is liable and is subject to service of process in a proceeding in this state for the enforcement of an obligation of a domestic corporation or a domestic business corporation which is a party to the merger or consolidation.

450.2737 Effect of merger or consolidation where surviving or new corporation is domestic corporation, domestic business corporation, or foreign business corporation.

Sec. 737.

If a surviving or new corporation is a domestic corporation to be governed by the laws of this state, the effect of the merger or consolidation authorized by section 736 is the same as in the case of a merger or consolidation of domestic corporations. If a surviving or new business corporation is a domestic business corporation to be governed by the laws of this state, the effect of a merger or consolidation is the same as in the case of a merger or consolidation of domestic business corporations, subject to Act No. 284 of the Public Acts of 1972, as amended. If a surviving or new business corporation is a foreign business corporation to be governed by the laws of a jurisdiction other than this state, the effect of the merger or consolidation is the same as in the case of the merger or consolidation in such jurisdiction, except as otherwise herein provided.

450.2741 Abandonment of merger or consolidation; certificate of abandonment.

Sec. 741.

At any time before the effective date of a certificate of merger or consolidation, the merger or consolidation may be abandoned pursuant to provisions therefor, if any, set forth in the plan of merger or consolidation. If a certificate of merger or consolidation has been filed by a corporation, it shall file a certificate of abandonment within 10 days after the abandonment, but not later than the proposed effective day.

450.2753 Disposition of property and assets of corporation; approval; notice of meeting; statement; authorization; fixing terms or conditions and consideration; voting; abandonment.

Sec. 753.

(1) A sale, lease, exchange, or other disposition of all, or substantially all, the property and assets, with or without the goodwill, of a corporation, may be made upon such terms and conditions and for a consideration, which may consist in whole or in part of cash or other property, including shares, bonds, or other securities of any other corporation or business corporation, domestic or foreign, as authorized as provided in this section.

(2) The board shall approve a proposal for the sale, lease, exchange, or other disposition.

(3) In the case of a stock or membership corporation, the proposed transaction shall be submitted for approval at a meeting of shareholders or members. Notice of the meeting shall be given to each shareholder or member of record whether or not entitled to vote at the meeting, not less than 20 days before the meeting, in the manner provided in this act for the giving of notice of meetings of shareholders or members. The notice shall include or be accompanied by a statement summarizing the principal terms of the proposed transaction or a copy of any documents containing the principal terms.

(4) At the meeting the shareholders or members may authorize the sale, lease, exchange, or other disposition and may fix, or may authorize the board to fix, any term or condition thereof and the consideration to be

received by the corporation therefor. The authorization requires the affirmative vote of the holders of a majority of the outstanding shares or members of the corporation entitled to vote thereon, and if a class is entitled to vote thereon as a class, the affirmative vote of a majority of the outstanding shares or members of each such class.

(5) Notwithstanding authorization by the shareholders or members, the board may abandon the sale, lease, exchange, or other disposition, subject to the rights of third parties under any contracts relating thereto without further action or approval by shareholders or members.

(6) In the case of a corporation organized upon a directorship basis, a sale, lease, exchange, or other disposition of all, or substantially all, the property and assets, with or without goodwill, of a corporation, shall be authorized upon receiving the affirmative vote of a majority of the directors then in office. Notice of the meeting to authorize the sale, lease, exchange, or other disposition shall be given to each director then in office not less than 20 days before the meeting and shall include a statement summarizing the principal terms of the proposed transaction or a copy of any documents containing the principal terms.

Chapter 8 – Dissolution

450.2801 Dissolution of corporation; methods; summary dissolution of corporation whose assets disposed of under court order in receivership or bankruptcy proceedings; filing copy of order with administrator.

Sec. 801.

(1) A corporation may be dissolved in any of the following ways:
   (a) Automatically by expiration of a period of duration to which the corporation is limited by its articles of incorporation.
   (b) By action of the incorporators or directors pursuant to section 803.
   (c) By action of the shareholders, members, or the board pursuant to section 804.
   (d) By action of a shareholder or member pursuant to section 805.
   (e) By a judgment of the circuit court in an action brought pursuant to this act or otherwise.
   (f) Automatically, pursuant to section 922, for failure to file an annual report or pay the annual filing fee or a penalty added to the fee.
(2) A corporation whose assets have been wholly disposed of under court order in receivership or bankruptcy proceedings may be summarily dissolved by order of the court having jurisdiction of the proceedings. A copy of the order shall be filed with the administrator by the clerk of the court.

450.2803 Dissolution of corporation by action of incorporators or directors; conditions; certificate of dissolution.

Sec. 803.

(1) A corporation may be dissolved by action of its incorporators or directors, if the corporation complies with all of the following conditions:
   (a) Has not commenced affairs.
   (b) Has not issued any shares and has no members entitled to vote on dissolution.
   (c) Has no debts or other liabilities.
   (d) Has received no payments on subscriptions for its shares or memberships, contributions or other funds from members or third

parties, or, if it has received payments, has returned them to those entitled thereto, less any part thereof disbursed for expenses.
(2) The dissolution of the corporation shall be effected by a majority of the incorporators or directors, executing and filing a certificate of dissolution stating:
   (a) The name of the corporation.
   (b) That the corporation has not commenced affairs, has issued no shares, and has no members entitled to vote on dissolution, and has no debts or other liabilities.
   (c) That the corporation has received no payments on subscriptions to its shares or memberships, contributions or other funds from members or third parties, or, if it has received payments, has returned them to those entitled thereto, less any part thereof disbursed for expenses.
   (d) That a majority of the incorporators or directors have elected that the corporation be dissolved.

450.2804 Dissolution of corporation by action of shareholders, members, or board; resolution; approval or authorization; notice; voting; certificate.

Sec. 804.

(1) A corporation may be dissolved by action of its shareholders, members, or board as provided in this section.
(2) The board shall adopt a resolution that the corporation be dissolved and that a plan of distribution of assets complying with section 855 be implemented.
(3) If the corporation is organized upon a stock or membership basis, the proposed dissolution shall be submitted for approval at a meeting of shareholders or members. Notice shall be given to each shareholder or member of record entitled to vote at the meeting as provided in this act for the giving of notice of meetings of shareholders or members, and shall state that a purpose of the meeting is to vote on dissolution of the corporation. The notice shall include a copy or summary of the plan of distribution of assets.
(4) At the meeting a vote of shareholders or members shall be taken on the proposed dissolution and plan of distribution of assets. The dissolution shall be approved upon receiving the affirmative vote of the holders of a majority of the outstanding shares or a majority of the members of the

corporation entitled to vote thereon, and if a class is entitled to vote thereon as a class, the affirmative vote of a majority of the outstanding shares or members of each such class.
(5) If the corporation is organized upon a directorship basis, the dissolution shall be authorized by the affirmative vote of a majority of directors then in office. Notice of the meeting to authorize the dissolution shall be given to each director then in office not less than 10 days before the meeting and shall state that a purpose of the meeting is to vote on dissolution of the corporation. The notice shall include a copy or summary of the plan of distribution of assets.
(6) If the dissolution is approved, a certificate of dissolution shall be executed and filed on behalf of the corporation, setting forth:
   (a) The name of the corporation.
   (b) The date and place of the meeting of shareholders, members, or directors approving the dissolution.
   (c) A statement that dissolution was approved by the requisite vote of directors and shareholders, directors and members, or directors.

450.2805 Provision in articles permitting shareholders, members, or directors to require dissolution authorized; plan of distribution of assets; execution and filing of certificate of dissolution; noting existence of provision on face of share certificates or membership certificates.

Sec. 805.

(1) The articles of incorporation may contain a provision that a shareholder, a member, or a director, or the holders of any specified number or proportion of shares or any specified number or proportion of members or directors, or of any specified number or proportion of shares or members of a class, may require dissolution of the corporation at will or upon the occurrence of a specified event, if all the incorporators have authorized the provision in the articles or the holders of record of all outstanding shares or all the members or all the directors authorize the provision in an amendment to the articles. Said provision shall also specify a plan of distribution of assets of the corporation which complies with section 855.
(2) If the articles contain this provision, dissolution may be effected by the execution and filing of a certificate of dissolution on behalf of the corporation when authorized by a holder or holders of the number or proportion of shares or by the number or proportion of members or

directors specified in the provision, obtained in such manner as may be specified therein, or if no manner is specified therein, when authorized on written consent signed by such holder or holders, member or members, or director or directors. The certificate of dissolution shall state the name of the corporation and that the corporation is dissolved pursuant to a designated provision in the articles.

(3) If the articles contain a provision authorized by subsection (1), the existence of the provision shall be noted conspicuously on the face of every certificate for shares issued by the corporation or on the face of a membership certificate delivered to every member of the corporation, and a holder or recipient of such certificate is conclusively deemed to have taken delivery or assumed membership with notice of the provision.

450.2811 Revocation of dissolution proceedings; resolution of board; approval; notice of meeting; voting; certificate of revocation.

Sec. 811.

(1) Dissolution proceedings commenced pursuant to section 804 or 805 may be revoked before complete distribution of assets, if a proceeding pursuant to section 851 is not pending, by filing a certificate of revocation executed, in person or by proxy, by all the shareholders, members, or directors entitled to vote on dissolution, stating that revocation is effective pursuant to this section and that all the shareholders, members, or directors of the corporation entitled to vote on dissolution have executed the certificate in person or by proxy.

(2) Dissolution proceedings commenced pursuant to section 804 may also be revoked before complete distribution of assets, if a proceeding pursuant to section 851 is not pending, in the following manner:

    (a) The board of directors shall adopt a resolution that the dissolution be revoked. The proposed revocation shall be submitted for approval at a meeting of shareholders, members, or directors, and the shareholders, members, or directors shall be given the same notice of the meeting and the revocation shall be approved by the same vote as that required by section 804 for the approval of dissolution.

    (b) A certificate of revocation, stating that dissolution is revoked pursuant to this section, and giving the information required by section 804(6), shall be executed and filed on behalf of the corporation.

450.2815 Renewal of corporate existence.

Sec. 815.

A corporation whose term has expired may renew its corporate existence, if a proceeding pursuant to section 851 is not pending, in the following manner:
(a) The board shall adopt a resolution that the corporate existence be renewed.
(b) If the corporation is organized upon a stock or membership basis, the proposed renewal shall be submitted for approval at a meeting of shareholders or members. Notice shall be given to each shareholder or member of record entitled to vote at the meeting within the time and in the manner provided in this act for the giving of notice of meetings of shareholders or members, and shall state that a purpose of the meeting is to vote on the renewal of corporate existence. At the meeting a vote of shareholders or members entitled to vote thereat shall be taken on the proposed renewal which shall be adopted upon receiving the affirmative vote of holders of a majority of the outstanding shares or a majority of the members of the corporation entitled to vote thereon, and if a class of shareholders or members is entitled to vote thereon as a class, the affirmative vote of a majority of the outstanding shares or the members of each such class. Unless a greater vote is required in the articles of incorporation or in a bylaw adopted by the shareholders or members, the proposed renewal shall also be adopted upon receiving an affirmative vote of a majority of members or shares of shareholders present in person or by proxy at such meeting if due notice of the time, place, and object of the meeting was given by mail, at last known address, to each shareholder or member entitled to vote thereon at least 20 days prior to the date of the meeting or by publication in a publication distributed to its shareholders or members at least 20 days prior to the date of the meeting.
(c) If the corporation is organized upon a directorship basis, renewal shall be authorized by the affirmative vote of a majority of directors then in office.
(d) If renewal of the corporate existence is approved, a certificate of renewal shall be executed and filed on behalf of the corporation, setting forth:
    (i) The name of the corporation.
    (ii) The date and place of the meeting of shareholders or members approving the renewal of existence, if any.

(iii) A statement that renewal was approved by the requisite vote of directors and shareholders, directors and members, or directors.

(iv) The duration of the corporation, if other than perpetual.

450.2817 Effect of filing certificate of revocation of dissolution or renewal of corporate existence; accrued penalty or liability; adoption of different name.

Sec. 817.

(1) Upon filing of the certificate of revocation of dissolution or of renewal of existence, the revocation of the dissolution proceedings or the renewal of the corporate existence becomes effective, and the corporation may again conduct affairs.
(2) Revocation of dissolution or renewal of corporate existence does not relieve the corporation of any penalty or liability accrued against it under any law of this state.
(3) If during the period of dissolution or expiration of term the corporate name or a confusingly similar name has been assigned to another corporation, the administrator may require that the corporation adopt a different name upon filing of a certificate of revocation of dissolution or of renewal of existence.

450.2821 Action by attorney general for dissolution of corporation; grounds.

Sec. 821.

(1) The attorney general may bring an action in the circuit court for the county in which the registered office of the corporation is located for dissolution of a corporation upon the ground that the corporation has committed any of the following acts:
   (a) Procured its organization through fraud.
   (b) Repeatedly and wilfully exceeded the authority conferred upon it by law.
   (c) Repeatedly and wilfully conducted its affairs in an unlawful manner.
(2) The enumeration in this section of grounds for dissolution does not exclude any other statutory or common law action by the attorney

general for dissolution of a corporation or revocation or forfeiture of its corporate franchises.

450.2823 Dissolution of corporation by judgment in action brought by director, shareholder, or member; proof.

Sec. 823.

A corporation may be dissolved by a judgment entered in an action brought in the circuit court for the county in which the registered office of the corporation is located by 1 or more directors or by 1 or more shareholders or members entitled to vote in an election of directors of the corporation, upon proof of both of the following:
(a) The directors of the corporation are unable to agree by the requisite vote on material matters respecting management of the corporation's affairs, or the shareholders or members of the corporation are so divided in voting power that they have failed to elect successors to any director whose term has expired or would have expired upon the election and qualification of the director's successor.
(b) As a result of a condition stated in subdivision (a), the corporation is unable to carry out its corporate purposes or function effectively in the best interests of its creditors and shareholders or members, if any.

450.2825 Adjudging dissolution and liquidation of assets and affairs of corporation by circuit court in action filed by shareholder, member, or director; grounds; making order or granting relief other than dissolution.

Sec. 825.

(1) The circuit court for the county in which the registered office of the corporation is located may adjudge the dissolution of, and liquidate the assets and affairs of, a corporation, in an action filed by a shareholder, member, or director when it is established that the acts of the directors or those in control of the corporation are illegal, fraudulent, or wilfully unfair and oppressive to the corporation or to such shareholder or member or contrary to the purposes of the corporation.
(2) In an action filed by a shareholder, member, or director to dissolve the corporation on a ground enumerated in subsection (1), the circuit court upon establishment of such ground may make such order or grant such

relief, other than dissolution, as it deems appropriate, including, without limitation, an order providing for any of the following:
  (a) Cancellation or alteration of a provision contained in the articles of incorporation, or an amendment thereof, or in the bylaws of the corporation.
  (b) Cancellation, alteration, or injunction against a resolution or other act of the corporation.
  (c) Direction or prohibition of an act of the corporation or of shareholders, members, directors, officers, or other persons party to the action.
  (d) In the case of shares which are transferable, purchase at their fair value of shares of a shareholder, either by the corporation or by the officers, directors, or other shareholders responsible for the wrongful acts.

450.2831 Dissolution of corporation; conditions.

Sec. 831.

A corporation is dissolved when any of the following occurs:
(a) The period of duration stated in the corporation's articles of incorporation expires.
(b) A certificate of dissolution is filed pursuant to sections 803 to 805.
(c) A judgment of forfeiture of corporate franchises or of dissolution is entered by a court of competent jurisdiction and a copy of a judicial order of dissolution shall be forwarded promptly to the administrator by the receiver or other person designated by the court.
(d) Failure to file an annual report or pay an annual filing fee, as provided in section 922.

450.2833 Dissolved corporation; continuation of corporate existence; conduct of affairs.

Sec. 833.

Except as a court may otherwise direct, a dissolved corporation shall continue its corporate existence but shall not conduct affairs except for the purpose of winding up its affairs by:
(a) Collecting its assets.

(b) Selling or otherwise transferring, with or without security, assets which are not to be distributed in kind pursuant to section 855.
(c) Paying its debts and other liabilities.
(d) Doing all other acts incident to liquidation of its affairs.

450.2834 Dissolved corporation and officers, directors, shareholders, and members; manner of functioning.

Sec. 834.

Subject to section 833 and except as otherwise provided by court order, a dissolved corporation, its officers, directors, shareholders, and members shall continue to function in the same manner as if dissolution had not occurred. Without limiting the generality of this section:
(a) The directors of the corporation are not deemed to be trustees of its assets solely because of the fact of dissolution and shall thereby be held to no greater standard of conduct than that prescribed by section 541.
(b) Title to the corporation's assets remains in the corporation until transferred by it in the corporate name.
(c) The dissolution does not change quorum or voting requirements for the board, shareholders, or members and does not alter provisions regarding election, appointment, resignation or removal of, or filling vacancies among, directors or officers, or provisions regarding amendment or repeal of bylaws or adoption of new bylaws.
(d) Shares may be transferred if otherwise authorized.
(e) The corporation may sue and be sued in its corporate name and process may issue by and against the corporation in the same manner as if dissolution had not occurred.
(f) An action brought against the corporation before its dissolution does not abate because of the dissolution.

450.2841 Notice to creditors; "creditor" defined.

Sec. 841.

(1) After a corporation has been dissolved, the corporation, or a receiver appointed for it pursuant to this chapter, may give notice requiring all creditors to present their claims in writing. The notice shall be published once in each of 3 consecutive weeks in a newspaper in the county in which the registered office of the corporation is located. The notice shall

state that all persons who are creditors of the corporation shall file their claims in writing with the corporation or the receiver at a place and on or before a date named in the notice, which date shall be not less than 6 months after the date of the first publication.

(2) As used in this section and sections 842 and 843, "creditor" means a person to whom the corporation is indebted, and any other person who has a claim or right against the corporation, liquidated or unliquidated, matured or unmatured, direct or indirect, absolute or contingent, secured or unsecured.

450.2842 Mailing notice to creditor of corporation; failure to file claim as bar to enforcement; applicability.

Sec. 842.

(1) On or before the date of first publication of the notice prescribed in section 841, the corporation or the receiver shall mail a copy of the notice to each known creditor of the corporation. The giving of the notice does not constitute recognition that a person to whom the notice is directed is a creditor of the corporation other than for the purpose of receipt of notice hereunder.

(2) Except as otherwise provided in this act, a creditor who does not file a claim as required by the notice, and all persons claiming through or under that creditor, are forever barred from suing on the claim or otherwise realizing upon or enforcing it. However, this section does not apply to a claim in litigation on the date of the first publication of the notice and does not preclude the enforcement of a lien, encumbrance, or other security interest. A claim filed by a trustee or paying agent for the holders of bonds or coupons has the same effect as if filed by the holder of any such bond or coupon.

450.2843 Rejection of claim filed by creditor; notice; failure to commence action as bar to enforcement of claim.

Sec. 843.

If the corporation, or the receiver of a corporation appointed pursuant to this chapter, rejects in whole or in part a claim filed by a creditor, the corporation or the receiver shall mail notice of the rejection to the creditor. The notice shall state that if the creditor does not commence an action on the claim within 60 days after the notice was mailed to the creditor, the creditor and all persons claiming through or under the creditor, except as otherwise provided in this chapter, are forever barred from suing on the claim or otherwise realizing upon or enforcing it. Failure to commence such an action is a bar to enforcement of the claim.

450.2851 Application for judgment that affairs of corporation and liquidation of assets continue under supervision of court; orders and judgments; permitting creditor to file claim or commence action.

Sec. 851.

(1) After a corporation has been dissolved in any manner, the corporation, a creditor, a shareholder, member, or a director may apply at any time to the circuit court for the county in which the registered office of the corporation is located for a judgment that the affairs of the corporation and the liquidation of its assets continue under supervision of the court. The court shall make such orders and judgments as may be required, including, but not limited to, continuance of the liquidation of the corporation's assets by its officers and directors under supervision of the court, or the appointment of a receiver of the corporation to be vested with powers as the court designates to liquidate the affairs of the corporation.

(2) For good cause shown, and so long as a corporation has not made complete distribution of its assets, the court, in an action pending under this section or otherwise, may permit a creditor who has not filed a claim within the time limited by section 841, or who has not commenced an action on a rejected claim within the time limited by section 842, to file such claim or to commence such action within such time as the court directs.

450.2855 Application and distribution of assets upon dissolution.

Sec. 855.

Upon dissolution, the assets of a corporation shall be applied and distributed as follows:

(a) All liabilities and obligations of the corporation shall be paid and discharged, or adequate provision shall be made therefor.

(b) Assets held by the corporation upon condition requiring return, transfer, or conveyance, which condition occurs by reason of the dissolution, shall be returned, transferred, or conveyed in accordance with such requirements.

(c) Assets received and held by the corporation subject to limitations permitting their use only for charitable, religious, eleemosynary, benevolent, educational, or similar purposes, but not held upon a condition requiring return, transfer, or conveyance by reason of the dissolution, shall be transferred or conveyed in accordance with any provisions in the articles of incorporation or bylaws which designate 1 or more recipients or a mechanism for determining 1 or more recipients which are domestic or foreign corporations, societies, or organizations, including governmental agencies, engaged in activities furthering such purposes. If the articles of incorporation or bylaws do not contain such provisions, such assets shall be transferred or conveyed to 1 or more domestic or foreign corporations, societies, or organizations, including governmental agencies, engaged in activities substantially similar to or consistent with those of the dissolving corporation.

(d) Other assets, if any, shall be distributed in accordance with provisions of the articles of incorporation or the bylaws which determine the distributive rights of shareholders or members, or any class or classes of shareholders or members, or provide for distribution to others.

(e) Any remaining assets may be distributed to such persons, societies, organizations, domestic or foreign corporations, or domestic or foreign business corporations, as may be specified in a plan of distribution adopted by the corporation.

(f) When there is no provision for the distribution of assets, the assets remaining after implementation of the provisions of this section shall escheat to the state.

450.2861 Plan of reorganization; action by directors, shareholders, or members not required to put plan into effect.

Sec. 861.

A corporation for which a plan of reorganization has been confirmed by the judgment of a court of competent jurisdiction pursuant to any applicable law of this state or the United States may put into effect and carry out the plan without action by its directors, shareholders, or members. Such action may be taken as directed in the judgment by the receiver or trustee of the corporation appointed in the reorganization proceedings, or by any other person designated by the court.

450.2862 Powers of corporation under reorganization; issuing shares of capital stock and bonds for consideration specified in plan of reorganization.

Sec. 862.

(1) The corporation, in the manner provided in section 861, but without limiting the generality or effect of that section, may amend or repeal its bylaws; constitute or reconstitute and classify or reclassify its board of directors, and name, constitute, or appoint directors and officers in place of or in addition to any director or officer then in office; amend its articles of incorporation, and make any change in its capital or capital stock, or any other amendment, change, alteration, or provision, authorized by this act; be dissolved, transfer any part of its assets, and merge or consolidate as permitted by this act, change the location of its registered office, and remove or appoint a resident agent; authorize and fix the terms, manner, and conditions of the issuance of bonds, debentures, or other obligations, whether or not convertible into shares of its capital stock of any class, or bearing warrants or other evidences of optional rights to purchase or subscribe for shares of its capital stock of any class, and lease its property and franchises.

(2) Irrespective of any other provision of this act, the corporation may issue its shares of capital stock and its bonds for the consideration specified in the plan of reorganization after confirmation of the plan.

450.2863 Document filed or recorded to accomplish corporate purpose pursuant to plan of reorganization; making, execution, and acknowledgment; contents; filing.

Sec. 863.

A certificate or other document required or permitted by law to be filed or recorded to accomplish any corporate purpose, sought to be accomplished pursuant to the plan of reorganization, shall be made, executed, and acknowledged, as may be directed by such judgment by the persons designated in section 861. The certificate or document shall certify that provision for the making of the certificate or document is contained in the plan of reorganization or in a judgment of a court having jurisdiction of the proceeding under such applicable statute of this state or of the United States for the reorganization of the corporation, and that the plan has been confirmed, as provided by such applicable statute, with the title and venue of the proceeding and the date of the judgment confirming the plan. The certificate or other document shall be filed as provided in section 131, and upon such filing becomes effective in accordance with the terms thereof and the provisions of sections 861 to 864.

450.2864 Reversal or vacation of reorganization plan; filing of other or further certificates or documents; effect; fees.

Sec. 864.

(1) If after the filing of a certificate or other document the order of confirmation of the plan of reorganization is reversed or vacated or the plan is modified, other or further certificates or documents shall be filed as required to conform to the plan of reorganization as finally confirmed or to the judgment of the court.
(2) Except as otherwise provided in sections 861 to 864, a certificate or other document filed pursuant to this section or section 863 is not deemed to confer on a corporation any power, privilege, or franchise, except those permitted to be conferred on a corporation formed or existing under this act.
(3) On the filing of a certificate or other document pursuant to this section or any other section of this act, the same fees shall be paid to the administrator as are payable by a corporation not in reorganization upon filing like certificates or documents.

Chapter 9 – Renewal and Reporting

450.2901 Report of corporation; contents; electronic transmission; distribution to shareholder, member, or director.

Sec. 901.

(1) Each domestic corporation at least once in each year shall cause a report of the corporation for the preceding fiscal year to be made and distributed to each shareholder or member thereof or presented at the annual meeting of shareholders or members, or, if the corporation is organized upon a directorship basis, at the annual meeting of the board. The report shall include the corporation's year-end statement of assets and liabilities, including trust funds, and the principal change in assets and liabilities during the year preceding the date of the report and, if prepared by the corporation, its source and application of funds and any other information required by this act.

(2) A corporation may distribute the financial report required under subsection (1) electronically, either by electronic transmission of the report or by making the report available for electronic transmission. If the report is distributed electronically under this subsection, the corporation shall provide the report in written form to a shareholder, member, or director on request.

450.2911 Annual report to administrator; filing; contents.

Sec. 911.

(1) A domestic or foreign corporation authorized to conduct affairs in this state shall file a report with the administrator no later than October 1 of each year. The report, on a form approved by the administrator, shall contain all of the following information:
   (a) The name of the corporation.
   (b) The name of resident agent and address of its registered office in this state.
   (c) The names and business or residence addresses of its officers and directors.
   (d) Purposes of the corporation.
   (e) Nature and kind of business in which the corporation has engaged during the year covered by the report.

(2) The report required under this section is not required to be filed in the year of incorporation or authorization by corporations that were formed or authorized to do business on or after January 1 and before October 1 of that year.

(3) If there are not changes in the information provided in the last filed report, the corporation shall certify that no changes in the required information have occurred since the last filed report. The certification shall be on a report provided by the administrator and filed no later than the date required in subsection (1).

450.2913 Destruction or disposition of certain records.

Sec. 913.

The county clerk may destroy the copies of the corporate documents of a corporation which were forwarded to the office of the county clerk in accordance with Act No. 327 of the Public Acts of 1931, as amended, being sections 450.62 to 450.192 of the Michigan Compiled Laws, and its predecessor act. The clerk may destroy or dispose of these records in accordance with section 5 of Act No. 271 of the Public Acts of 1913, as amended, being section 399.5 of the Michigan Compiled Laws.

450.2922 Failure of domestic or foreign corporation to file annual report or pay filing fee; automatic dissolution or revocation of certificate of authority; dissolution of charitable purpose corporation; notice; right to certificate of good standing.

Sec. 922.

(1) If a domestic corporation neglects or refuses for 2 consecutive years to file the annual reports or pay the annual filing fee required by law, the corporation shall be automatically dissolved. The administrator shall notify the corporation of the impending dissolution not later than 90 days before the 2 years has expired. Until a corporation has been dissolved, it is entitled to issuance by the administrator, upon request, of a certificate of good standing setting forth that it has been validly incorporated as a domestic corporation and that it is validly in existence under the laws of this state.

(2) A charitable purpose corporation that is dissolved under subsection (1) shall provide notice of the dissolution to the attorney general within 60

days after the date of the dissolution and shall not dispose of any of its assets without written approval of the attorney general.

(3) If a foreign corporation neglects or refuses for 1 year to file the annual report or pay the annual filing fee required by law, its certificate of authority is subject to revocation in accordance with section 1042. Until revocation of its certificate of authority or its withdrawal from this state or termination of its existence, the foreign corporation is entitled to issuance by the administrator, upon request, of a certificate of good standing setting forth that it has been validly authorized to transact business in this state and that it holds a valid certificate of authority to transact business in this state.

450.2923 Extension of time for filing report; reporting failure or neglect under MCL 450.2922, 450.2931, and 450.2932 to attorney general; action by attorney general; certificate of mailing as evidence.

Sec. 923.

(1) The administrator for good cause shown may extend the time for filing of a report for not more than 1 year from the due date of the filing.
(2) The administrator may report promptly to the attorney general any failure or neglect under sections 922, 931, and 932, and the attorney general may commence an action for imposition of the prescribed penalties. When a corporation neglects or refuses to file its report within 90 days after the time prescribed by this act, the administrator shall notify the corporation of that fact by mail directed to its registered office. The administrator's certificate of mailing of the notice is prima facie evidence in all courts and places of that fact, and that the notice was received by the corporation.

450.2924 Annual reports due or deficient prior to date of act; penalties.

Sec. 924.

Annual reports due or deficient prior to the date of this act shall be subject to the penalties in effect at the statutory filing date.

450.2925 Renewal of corporate existence or certificate of authority following dissolution or revocation.

Sec. 925.

(1) A domestic corporation which has been dissolved pursuant to section 922(1), or a foreign corporation whose certificate of authority has been revoked pursuant to section 922(2) or section 1042, may renew its corporate existence or its certificate of authority by filing the reports for the last 5 years or any lesser number of years in which the reports were not filed and paying the annual filing fees for all the years for which they were not paid, together with a penalty of $5.00 for each delinquent report. Upon filing the reports and payment of the fees and penalties, the corporate existence or the certificate of authority is renewed. If during the intervening period the corporate name or a confusingly similar name has been assigned to another corporation, the administrator may require that the corporation adopt or use within this state a different name.
(2) Upon compliance with the provisions of this section, the rights of the corporation shall be the same as though a dissolution or revocation had not taken place, and all contracts entered into and other rights acquired during the interval shall be valid and enforceable.

450.2931 Wilful false statement in report; additional penalty.

Sec. 931.

If a domestic or foreign corporation which is required to file a report as provided in section 911 wilfully makes a false statement in the report, it is subject to an additional penalty of $1,000.00.

450.2932 Prohibited conduct as misdemeanor; fine.

Sec. 932.

(1) A person who knowingly makes or files or a person who knowingly assists in the making or filing of a false or fraudulent report, certificate, or other statement required by this act to be filed by a corporation with a public officer of this state, or a person knowing the same to be false or fraudulent, who procures, counsels, or advises the making or filing of such a report, certificate, or statement, is guilty of a misdemeanor and is subject to a fine of not to exceed $1,000.00 for each such offense.
(2) An officer or agent of a corporation who knowingly falsifies or wrongfully alters the books, records, or accounts of a corporation is

guilty of a misdemeanor and is subject to a fine of not to exceed $1,000.00 for each such offense.

450.2935 Authorizing, signing, or making false statement or notice; authorizing or making wrongful alteration of book, record, or account; liability; commencement of action.

Sec. 935.

(1) If a report, certificate, or other statement made, or public notice given by, the officers or directors of a corporation is false in a material representation, or if any book, record, or account of the corporation is knowingly or wrongfully altered, the officers, directors, or agents knowingly or wrongfully authorizing, signing, or making the false report, certificate, other statement or notice or authorizing or making the wrongful alteration are jointly and severally personally liable to a person who has become a creditor, shareholder, or member of the corporation upon the faith of the false material representation or alteration therein for all damages resulting therefrom.
(2) An action for the liability imposed by this section shall be commenced within 2 years after discovery of the false representation or alteration and within 6 years after the certificate, report, public notice, or other statement or the alteration has been made or given by the officers, directors, or agents of the corporation.

Chapter 10 – Foreign Corporations and Misc. Provisions

450.3001 Foreign corporation authorized to conduct affairs in this state on effective date of act; rights and privileges; duties, restrictions, penalties, and liabilities.

Sec. 1001.

A foreign corporation which is authorized to conduct affairs in this state on the effective date of this act, for a purpose for which a corporation might secure such authority under this act, has the rights and privileges applicable to a foreign corporation which receives a certificate of authority to transact business in this state under this act. From the effective date of this act the corporation is subject to the duties, restrictions, penalties, and liabilities prescribed herein for a foreign corporation which receives a certificate of authority to transact business in this state under this act.

450.3002 Foreign corporation receiving certificate of authority under act; rights and privileges; duties, restrictions, penalties, and liabilities.

Sec. 1002.

A foreign corporation which receives a certificate of authority under this act, until a certificate of revocation or of withdrawal is issued as provided in this act, has the same rights and privileges as a domestic corporation organized for the purposes set forth in the application pursuant to which the certificate of authority is issued. Except as otherwise provided in this act, the corporation is subject to the same duties, restrictions, penalties, and liabilities now or hereafter imposed upon a domestic corporation of like character.

450.3003 Foreign corporation conducting affairs without certificate of authority; duties, restrictions, penalties, and liabilities.

Sec. 1003.

A foreign corporation which conducts affairs in this state without a certificate of authority under this act is subject to the same duties, restrictions, penalties, and liabilities now or hereafter imposed upon a foreign corporation which receives such certificate of authority, in addition to any other penalty or liability imposed by law.

450.3011 Foreign corporation; certificate of authority required; extent of authorization to conduct affairs in state.

Sec. 1011.

A foreign corporation shall not conduct affairs in this state until it has procured a certificate of authority so to do from the administrator. A foreign corporation may be authorized to conduct affairs in this state which may be conducted lawfully in this state by a domestic corporation, to the extent that it is authorized to conduct such affairs in the jurisdiction where it is organized, but no other affairs.

450.3012 Foreign corporation not considered to be conducting affairs in state; activities; applicability of section.

Sec. 1012.

(1) Without excluding other activities which may not constitute conducting affairs in this state, a foreign corporation is not considered to be conducting affairs in this state, for the purposes of this act, solely because it is carrying on in this state any 1 or more of the following activities:
   (a) Maintaining or defending an action or suit or an administrative or arbitrative proceeding, or effecting the settlement thereof or the settlement of a claim or dispute.
   (b) Holding meetings of its directors, shareholders, or members or carrying on any other activities concerning its internal affairs.
   (c) Maintaining a bank account.
   (d) Effecting sales through an independent contractor.
   (e) Soliciting or procuring orders, whether by mail or through employees or agents or otherwise, where such orders require acceptance without this state before becoming binding contracts.
   (f) Borrowing money, with or without security.
   (g) Securing or collecting debts or enforcing any right in property securing the same.
   (h) Transacting any business in interstate commerce.
   (i) Conducting an isolated transaction not in the course of a number of repeated transactions of like nature.

(2) This section does not apply in determining the contracts or activities which may subject a foreign corporation to service of process or taxation in this state or to regulation under any other act of this state.

450.3015 Application of foreign corporation for certificate of authority to conduct affairs in state; contents.

Sec. 1015.

To procure a certificate of authority to conduct affairs in this state, a foreign corporation shall file with the administrator an application setting forth:
(a) The name of the corporation and the jurisdiction of its incorporation.
(b) The date of incorporation and the period of duration of the corporation.
(c) The street address, and the mailing address if different from the street address, of its main business or headquarters office.
(d) The address of its registered office in this state, and the name of its resident agent in this state at such address, together with a statement that the resident agent is an agent of the corporation upon whom process against the corporation may be served.
(e) The character of the affairs it is to transact in this state, together with a statement that it is authorized to conduct such affairs in the jurisdiction of its incorporation.
(f) Such additional information as the administrator may require in order to determine whether the corporation is entitled to a certificate of authority to conduct affairs in this state.

450.3016 Application of foreign corporation for certificate of authority to conduct affairs in state; attachments; fees; issuance of certificate; duration of authority.

Sec. 1016.

(1) A copy of the articles of incorporation and all amendments thereto, certified by the proper officer of the jurisdiction of its incorporation shall be attached to the application of a foreign corporation. A certificate setting forth that the corporation is in good standing under the laws of the jurisdiction of its incorporation, executed by the official of the jurisdiction who has custody of the records pertaining to corporations and dated not earlier than 30 days before filing of the application, shall also be attached to the application. If such certificate is in a foreign

language, a translation thereof under oath of the translator shall be attached thereto.

(2) Upon filing of the application, accompanied by the filing and franchise fees prescribed by law, the administrator shall issue to the foreign corporation a certificate of authority to conduct affairs in this state. Thereupon the foreign corporation is authorized to conduct in this state any affairs of the character set forth in its application. The authority continues so long as the foreign corporation retains its authority to conduct such affairs in the jurisdiction of its incorporation and its authority to conduct affairs in this state has not been surrendered, suspended, or revoked.

450.3021 Foreign corporation authorized to conduct affairs in state; filing with administrator copy of amendment of articles or certificate of merger, consolidation, or similar corporate action.

Sec. 1021.

(1) When the articles of incorporation of a foreign corporation authorized to conduct affairs in this state are amended, the foreign corporation, within 60 days after the amendment is effective, shall file with the administrator a copy of the amendment certified by the proper officers of the jurisdiction of its incorporation.

(2) When a foreign corporation authorized to conduct affairs in this state is a party to a merger, consolidation, or similar corporate action taken in accordance with the laws of the jurisdiction of its incorporation, the foreign corporation, within 60 days after the effective date thereof, shall file with the administrator a copy of the certificate of merger, consolidation, or similar corporate action, certified by the proper officers of the jurisdiction of its incorporation.

450.3031 Foreign corporation authorized to conduct affairs in state; withdrawal; certificate; application.

Sec. 1031.

A foreign corporation authorized to conduct affairs in this state may withdraw from this state upon receiving from the administrator a certificate of withdrawal. The foreign corporation shall file an application for withdrawal setting forth:

(a) The name of the corporation and the jurisdiction of its incorporation.
(b) That the corporation is not conducting affairs in this state.
(c) That the corporation surrenders its authority to conduct affairs in this state.

450.3032 Issuance of certificate of withdrawal; conditions; effect.

Sec. 1032.

Upon filing the application for withdrawal and payment of the filing fees prescribed by law, the administrator shall issue to the corporation a certificate of withdrawal, whereupon:
(a) The authority of the corporation to conduct affairs in this state shall cease.
(b) The authority of its resident agent in this state to accept service of process against the corporation is deemed revoked.

450.3035 Foreign corporation authorized to conduct affairs in state; termination or cancellation of authority or existence; filing information, certificate, order, or judgment with administrator; payment of fees; certificate of withdrawal.

Sec. 1035.

(1) When a foreign corporation authorized to conduct affairs in this state is dissolved, or its authority or existence is otherwise terminated or canceled in the jurisdiction of its incorporation, or it is merged into or consolidated with another corporation, there shall be filed with the administrator such information as may be required by the administrator to determine and assess any unpaid fees payable by such foreign corporation as required by law and either of the following:
   (a) A certificate of the official of the jurisdiction of incorporation of the foreign corporation who has custody of the records pertaining to corporations, evidencing the occurrence of any such event.
   (b) A certified copy of an order or judgment of a court of competent jurisdiction directing dissolution of the foreign corporation, the termination of its existence, or the cancellation of its authority.
   (c) Upon filing of the certificate, order, or judgment and payment of the filing fees prescribed by law, the administrator shall issue a

certificate of withdrawal with like effect as provided in section 1032.

450.3041 Revocation of certificate of authority of foreign corporation to conduct affairs in state; grounds.

Sec. 1041.

In addition to any other ground for revocation provided by law, the administrator may revoke the certificate of authority of a foreign corporation to conduct affairs in this state upon the conditions prescribed in section 1042 upon any of the following grounds:
(a) The corporation fails to maintain a resident agent in this state as required by this act.
(b) The corporation, after change of its registered office or resident agent, fails to file a statement of such change as required by this act.
(c) The corporation, after amending its articles of incorporation, fails to file a copy of the amendment as required by this act.
(d) The corporation, after becoming a party to a merger, consolidation, or similar corporation action, fails to file a copy of the certificate of merger, consolidation, or similar corporate action as required by this act.
(e) The corporation fails to file its annual report within the time required by this act.

450.3042 Revocation of certificate of authority of foreign corporation to conduct affairs in state; notice of default under MCL 450.3031; certificate of revocation.

Sec. 1042.

(1) The administrator shall revoke a certificate of authority of a foreign corporation only when the administrator has given the corporation not less than 90 days' notice that a default under section 922 exists and that its certificate of authority will be revoked unless the default is cured within 90 days after mailing of the notice, and the corporation fails before revocation to cure the default.
(2) The notice shall be sent by first class mail to the corporation at its registered office in this state and at its main business or headquarters office as these offices are on record in the office of the administrator.

(3) Upon revoking such a certificate of authority, the administrator shall issue a certificate of revocation and mail a copy to the corporation at each of the addresses designated in subsection (2).

(4) The issuance of the certificate of revocation has the same force and effect as issuance of a certificate of withdrawal under section 1031.

450.3051 Action commenced by foreign corporation without certificate of authority prohibited; applicability of prohibition; effect of failure to obtain certificate of authority on validity of contract and act of corporation; defense of action or proceeding.

Sec. 1051.

(1) A foreign corporation conducting affairs in this state without a certificate of authority shall not maintain an action or proceeding in any court of this state until the corporation has obtained a certificate of authority. An action commenced by a foreign corporation having no certificate of authority shall not be dismissed if a certificate of authority has been obtained before the order of dismissal. This prohibition applies to:
   (a) A successor in interest of the foreign corporation, except a receiver, trustee in bankruptcy, or other representative of creditors of the corporation.
   (b) An assignee of the foreign corporation, except an assignee for value who accepts an assignment without knowledge that the foreign corporation should have but has not obtained a certificate of authority in this state.
(2) Failure of a foreign corporation to obtain a certificate of authority to conduct affairs in this state does not impair the validity of a contract or act of the corporation, and does not prevent the corporation from defending an action or proceeding in a court of this state.

450.3055 Foreign corporation conducting affairs in state without certificate of authority; penalty.

Sec. 1055.

In addition to any other liability imposed by law, a foreign corporation conducting affairs in this state without a certificate of authority shall forfeit to the state a penalty of not less than $100.00 nor more than $1,000.00 for each calendar month, not more than 5 years prior thereto, in which it has conducted affairs in this state without a certificate of authority. This penalty shall not exceed $10,000.00. The penalty shall be recovered with costs in an action prosecuted by the attorney general.

450.3060 Fees; payment; certification of file or record; refund; waiver.

Sec. 1060.

(1) The fees a person shall pay to the administrator for the purposes described in this section are as follows:
   (a) Examining, filing, and copying of articles of a domestic corporation, $10.00.
   (b) Examining and filing articles or certificate of incorporation, and other papers connected with the application of a foreign corporation for admission to conduct affairs in this state, $10.00.
   (c) Examining, filing, and copying an amendment to the articles of a domestic corporation, $10.00.
   (d) Examining and filing an amendment to the articles of a foreign corporation, $10.00.
   (e) Examining, filing, and copying a certificate of merger or consolidation under chapter 7, $50.00.
   (f) Examining and filing a certificate of merger or consolidation of a foreign corporation, under section 1021, $10.00.
   (g) Examining, filing, and copying a certificate of dissolution, $10.00.
   (h) Examining and filing an application for withdrawal and issuance of a certificate of withdrawal of a foreign corporation, $10.00.
   (i) Examining, filing, and copying an application for reservation of corporate name, $10.00.
   (j) Examining, filing, and copying a certificate of assumed name or certificate of termination of assumed name, $10.00.
   (k) Examining, filing, and copying a statement of change of registered office or resident agent, $5.00.
   (l) Examining, filing, and copying restated articles of domestic corporation, $10.00.
   (m) Examining, filing, and copying a certificate of abandonment, $10.00.
   (n) Examining, filing, and copying a certificate of correction, $10.00.
   (o) Examining, filing, and copying a certificate of revocation of dissolution proceedings, $10.00.

- (p) Examining, filing, and copying a certificate of renewal of corporate existence, $10.00.
- (q) Filing and examination of a special report required by law, $2.00.
- (r) Examining and filing a certificate of election, $10.00.
- (s) Filing a report required under section 911, $10.00 if paid before October 1, 2003 or after September 30, 2015. After September 30, 2003 and before October 1, 2015, the fee is $20.00.

(2) A corporation shall pay the applicable fee described in this section to the administrator at the time of filing or when the service is rendered by the administrator. The fees described in this section are in addition to any franchise fees prescribed in this act.

(3) A person shall pay a minimum charge of $1.00 for each certificate and 50 cents per folio to the administrator for certifying a part of a file or record pertaining to a corporation if a fee for that service is not described in subsection (1). The administrator may furnish copies of documents, reports, and papers required or permitted by law to be filed with the administrator, and shall charge for those copies the fee established in a schedule of fees adopted by the administrator with the approval of the state administrative board.

(4) The administrator shall not refund all or any part of a fee described in this section. The administrator shall deposit all fees received and collected under this section in the state treasury to the credit of the administrator, who may only use the money credited pursuant to legislative appropriation and only in carrying out those duties of the department required by law.

(5) The administrator shall waive any fee otherwise required under this section if a majority of the members or directors of the corporation responsible for paying the fee are, and the corporation provides proof satisfactory to the administrator that a majority of the members or directors are, honorably discharged veterans of the armed forces of the United States.

450.3061 Fee for privilege of exercising franchises in state.

Sec. 1061.

Every corporation organized or conducting affairs in this state shall, upon filing its articles, or, if a foreign corporation, upon filing its application for admission, pay to the administrator a fee of $10.00 for the privilege of exercising its franchises within this state, upon such organization or admission as the case may be.

450.3098 Repeal of acts and parts of acts.

Sec. 1098.

The following acts and parts of acts are repealed:
(a) Act No. 213 of the Public Acts of 1935, being sections 450.401 to 450.402 of the Compiled Laws of 1970.
(b) Act No. 90 of the Public Acts of 1954, being sections 450.441 to 450.442 of the Compiled Laws of 1970.
(c) Sections 62, 63, 64, 81, 92, 117, 118, 119, 119a, 120, 121, 122, 123, 124, 124a, 125, 126, 127, 128, 129, 130, 131, 132, 132a, 163, 164, 165, 166, 167, 168, 188, and 189 of Act No. 327 of the Public Acts of 1931, as amended, being sections 450.62, 450.63, 450.64, 450.81, 450.92, 450.117, 450.118, 450.119, 450.119a, 450.120, 450.121, 450.122, 450.123, 450.124, 450.124a, 450.125, 450.126, 450.127, 450.128, 450.129, 450.130, 450.131, 450.132, 450.132a, 450.163, 450.164, 450.165, 450.166, 450.167, 450.168, 450.188, and 450.189 of the Compiled Laws of 1970.
(d) Act No. 161 of the Public Acts of 1947, being sections 450.421 to 450.422 of the Compiled Laws of 1970.

450.3099 Effective date of act.

Sec. 1099.

This act shall take effect January 1, 1983.

Chapter 11 – Cooperatives

450.3100 Short title.

Sec. 1100.

This chapter shall be known and may be cited as the "consumer cooperative act".

450.3101 Applicability of act and chapter; amendment of articles or bylaws; exemption.

Sec. 1101.

(1) Except as otherwise provided in this act or by other law, this act and this chapter apply to:
 (a) All consumer cooperatives which are organized after the effective date of this amendatory act.
 (b) All consumer cooperatives which have been organized under this act, a predecessor act, or other act and which have represented themselves to be cooperatives.
 (c) All other corporations that elect to accept this act pursuant to section 1192.
 (d) All other cooperatives organized under this chapter.
 (e) All foreign cooperatives to the extent provided in sections 1123 and 1191.
(2) A consumer cooperative which was organized under a predecessor or other act is subject to this act and this chapter except to the extent that either conflicts with the articles, bylaws, or cooperative plan of the consumer cooperative lawfully made pursuant to the predecessor or other act. The consumer cooperative may amend its articles or bylaws to bring itself in conformity with this act. If a corporation elects to accept this act and this chapter pursuant to section 1192, the corporation shall amend its articles and bylaws, as necessary, to bring itself in conformity with this act and this chapter.
(3) A nonprofit power corporation as described in section 261(4) may elect to be exempted from this chapter by the effective date of this amendatory act by a resolution of the board of directors of the corporation. If such a corporation should subsequently elect to accept this act and this chapter pursuant to section 1192, the corporation shall amend its articles and

bylaws, as necessary, to bring itself in conformity with this act and this chapter.
(4) This chapter shall not apply to a cooperative organized substantially for the purpose of agricultural production, processing, supply, research, bargaining, or marketing which is organized under sections 98 to 109 of Act No. 327 of the Public Acts of 1931, being sections 450.98 to 450.109 of the Michigan Compiled Laws, or a farm cooperative the majority of votes of which are held by farmers, unless the cooperative elects to accept this chapter pursuant to section 1192.

450.3102 Controlling definitions.

Sec. 1102.

The definitions contained in sections 1103 and 1104 shall control in the interpretation of this chapter, unless the context otherwise requires.

450.3103 Definitions; C to F.

Sec. 1103.

(1) "Consumer" means a natural person who acquires, or commits to acquire in the future from the cooperative primarily for consumption, use, or occupancy by the person or the person's family, any of the goods, services, or facilities furnished by the cooperative.
(2) "Consumer cooperative" means a cooperative the majority of the votes of which are held by consumers, or, in the case of a cooperative which provides residential dwelling units, the majority of the votes of which are held by consumers and the majority of members of which do not have the right of possession or occupancy of dwelling units they do not occupy.
(3) "Cooperative" means a corporation organized on a cooperative basis or similar basis that is provided in law as a criterion for being a cooperative.
(4) "Cooperative basis" means:
 (a) That, subject to section 1133, each member has 1 vote, except as provided in this chapter.
 (b) That the dividends, if any, paid on member capital do not exceed 8% per year.
 (c) That the net savings are distributed as provided in section 1135.
 (d) That business is engaged in for the mutual benefit of its members.

(5) "Electronic transmission" or "electronically transmitted" means any form of communication that meets all of the following:
   (a) It does not directly involve the physical transmission of paper.
   (b) It creates a record that may be retained and retrieved by the recipient.
   (c) It may be directly reproduced in paper form by the recipient through an automated process.
(6) "Foreign cooperative" means a corporation organized under laws other than the laws of this state operating on a cooperative basis or a similar basis that is provided in those other laws as a criterion for being a cooperative.

450.3104 Definitions; M to U.

Sec. 1104.

(1) "Member capital" means the assets which a member must provide by payment, transfer, or allocation of net savings to a cooperative as a condition of admission to or retention of membership and with respect to which the member has rights to dividends, redemption or distributions on dissolution pursuant to this chapter.
(2) "Membership fee" means a nonredeemable fee which a member must pay to a cooperative as a condition of admission to or retention of membership in the cooperative which is not member capital or a fee for goods, services, or facilities.
(3) "Patron" means a person whose economic exchange is a regular part of the business of a cooperative or foreign cooperative, which economic exchange is the same type of regular economic exchange engaged in by any class of members.
(4) "Patronage" means the selling or providing of goods, services, or facilities to, or the buying of goods, services, or facilities from members or other persons, or the providing of labor or services to or by a cooperative.
(5) "Redemption" means any method by which a cooperative exchanges cash or debt instruments for member capital, including, but not limited to, repurchase, redemption, refund, or repayment.
(6) "Referendum" means a method of member voting that utilizes secret ballot and established polling places as provided in the cooperative's bylaws.
(7) "Unincorporated cooperative" means either of the following:

(a) An association of 2 or more persons organized on a cooperative basis which is not a corporation.

(b) An association of 2 or more persons organized under the laws of another state operating on either a cooperative basis or a similar basis provided in another state as the criterion for being a cooperative, which is not a corporation.

450.3107 Inconsistent provisions inapplicable to chapter.

Sec. 1107.

To the extent that sections 301(3) and (4), 855, and 901 are inconsistent with this chapter, they shall not apply to cooperatives.

450.3109 Requirements of MCL 460.1 et seq. not modified; effect of economic activity conducted by cooperative.

Sec. 1109.

(1) This chapter does not modify the requirements of Act No. 3 of the Public Acts of 1939, being sections 460.1 to 460.8 of the Michigan Compiled Laws.
(2) The fact that a cooperative conducts economic activity under this act shall not alone cause the economic activity of the cooperative to be considered a conspiracy or combination in restraint of trade or an illegal monopoly, or an attempt to lessen competition or fix prices arbitrarily.

450.3121 Articles of incorporation; requirement.

Sec. 1121.

In addition to the requirements of section 202, the articles of incorporation of a cooperative organized under this act shall state whether the cooperative will be financed on a membership fee basis, a member capital basis, or a combination of both.

450.3123 Use of term "cooperative," "co-op," "consumer cooperative," or any variation thereof.

Sec. 1123.

(1) The term "cooperative", "co-op", or any variation thereof, may only be used in the name of cooperatives organized under or subject to this chapter, corporations organized under or subject to sections 98 to 109 of Act No. 327 of the Public Acts of 1931, being sections 450.98 to 450.109 of the Michigan Compiled Laws, parent cooperative preschools licensed under Act No. 116 of the Public Acts of 1973, being sections 722.111 to 722.128 of the Michigan Compiled Laws, credit unions chartered under the laws of this state or federal law, corporations organized on a cooperative basis or similar basis and organized before the effective date of this amendatory act as nonprofit corporations, unincorporated cooperatives, foreign cooperatives, any entities wholly owned by any of the foregoing or any combination of such entities, and any other entities specifically authorized by statute to use "cooperative", "co-op", or any variation thereof.

(2) The term "consumer cooperative" or any variation thereof may only be used in the name of a consumer cooperative or a foreign or unincorporated cooperative the majority of the votes of which are held by consumers and which complies with sections 1132 and 1138.

(3) Unless authorized by subsection (1) or (2), or as otherwise specifically provided by law, a person shall not use the term "cooperative", "co-op", "consumer cooperative", or any variation thereof, as part of a corporate or other business name or title.

(4) This section shall not be construed to authorize any use of the term "co-op", "cooperative", "consumer cooperative", or any variation thereof, that is prohibited by the cooperative identity protection act.

450.3125 Adoption of initial bylaws; ratification or amendment; contents of bylaws.

Sec. 1125.

(1) Notwithstanding section 231, the initial bylaws of a cooperative may be adopted by the incorporators, the board, or the members. If initial bylaws are adopted by the incorporators or the board, at the first meeting of members the bylaws shall be submitted to the members for ratification or amendment.

(2) Bylaws may contain provisions for educational programs for directors, members, employees, patrons, prospective members, and the community

and provisions for cooperative relations with cooperatives and unincorporated cooperatives.

450.3131 Organization on nonstock membership basis.

Sec. 1131.

Notwithstanding section 302, a cooperative organized under this act shall be organized on a nonstock membership basis and shall not be organized on a stock or directorship basis.

450.3132 Membership; notice of qualifications.

Sec. 1132.

Subject to section 304(7), membership in a consumer cooperative subject to this act shall be available to all patrons of the cooperative who are consumers. The bylaws may make membership available to other patrons. For any other cooperative, 50% or more of the patronage shall be with members or, subject to section 304(7), membership shall be available to all patrons. All cooperatives shall give all patrons reasonable notice of the qualifications for membership.

450.3133 Classification.

Sec. 1133.

If a cooperative has classes of members pursuant to section 304, classification shall be based only on 1 or more of the following number of members, number of persons served, type of patronage, level of patronage, or whether or not members are patrons. In a consumer cooperative, classification of consumers by level of patronage shall not be used.

450.3134 Cooperative organized on member capital basis, member fee basis, or basis combining member capital and membership fee; powers.

Sec. 1134.

(1) A cooperative which is organized on a member capital basis or on a basis combining member capital and membership fee may provide for any of the following, if such provision is set forth in the articles or bylaws:
  (a) A maximum member capital to be held by any 1 member.
  (b) Transfer of member capital pursuant to section 304(6).
  (c) Mandatory contribution or contributions of member capital as a condition or conditions of admission to or retention of membership, including but not limited to initial capital contributions, surcharges, and distributions of net savings pursuant to section 1135.
  (d) A dividend on membership capital, not to exceed 8% per year.
  (e) Special assessments on members.
(2) A cooperative which is organized on a membership fee basis or on a basis combining member capital and membership fee may provide for either or both of the following as a condition or conditions of admission to or retention of membership in the cooperative, if such a provision is set forth in its articles or bylaws:
  (a) The charging of a nonredeemable initial or periodic membership fee or fees.
  (b) Nonredeemable special assessments on members.

450.3135 Net savings; determination, allocation, distribution, and use; apportionment of losses.

Sec. 1135.

(1) At least once each year, a cooperative shall determine its net savings by deducting from total income:
  (a) All operating costs and expenses.
  (b) Reasonable reserves for depreciation and obsolescence of property, doubtful accounts, other valuation or operating reserves, capital investments and reserves for capital investment.
  (c) Dividends paid on member capital and interest or dividends paid on nonvoting investment certificates or bonds, if any.
(2) The articles or bylaws may provide for any reasonable method of allocating net savings by the board of directors for the common benefit of all the patrons of a cooperative.
(3) Unless the articles or bylaws otherwise provide pursuant to subsection (2), net savings shall be allocated, distributed, or used in any of the following ways:

(a) By allocation of net savings to all patrons at a uniform rate in proportion to their individual patronage, provided that different rates of allocation may be established according to the net savings generated by various departments or types of business done by the cooperative. Distribution to patrons may be made as follows:
  (i) In cash or credits. Credits shall be evidenced by shares, revolving fund certificates, notices of allocation, capital credits, or other certificates or notices of the cooperative, or any combination thereof.
  (ii) In the case of nonmember patrons who have subscribed for membership, distribution may be credited toward payment of unpaid member capital or membership fees.
  (iii) In the case of nonmember patrons, distribution of the proportionate amount of net savings generated by nonmember patronage may be made to a general fund. Redistribution shall be made to an individual nonmember patron only upon request and presentation of evidence of the nonmember's patronage. Such net savings may be distributed in cash or credited toward payment of member capital or membership fees. Reasonable notice shall be provided to nonmember patrons of their rights to redistribution and the means of applying for membership.
(b) By allocation to retained earnings, operating costs or capital expenditures of the cooperative to reduce the costs of goods, facilities, or services, to improve the quality provided or otherwise to further the common benefit of the patrons.
(4) The articles or bylaws may include any reasonable provisions for the apportionment of losses.

450.3136 Certificate; issuance; contents; restrictions on dividends.

Sec. 1136.

(1) If a cooperative is to be financed in whole or in part on a member capital basis, each member shall be provided a certificate or certificates setting forth the initial member capital of the member.
(2) A certificate issued pursuant to this section shall contain the information required by section 1138. The certificate may be denominated a membership certificate, share certificate, stock certificate, or a similar designation but shall not constitute shares as defined in section 109.

(3) The board of directors shall not pay dividends when currently the cooperative is insolvent or would thereby be made insolvent, or when the declaration, payment, or distribution of a dividend would be contrary to the articles or bylaws.

450.3137 Nonvoting investment certificate or bond.

Sec. 1137.

Subject to the uniform securities act, 1964 PA 265, MCL 451.501 to 451.818, and the uniform securities act (2002), 2008 PA 551, MCL 451.2101 to 451.2703, a cooperative may offer to its members or to the general public any form of nonvoting investment certificate or bond that may bear interest or dividends as provided by the board of directors.

450.3138 Advising persons in writing; statement on membership certificate.

Sec. 1138.

Prior to accepting a person as a member or any membership fee or member capital, a cooperative shall advise the person in writing of the items in subdivisions (a) to (g). A cooperative shall also conspicuously state on each membership certificate the items in subdivisions (a), (e), and (f)

(a) A statement that the corporation is a cooperative subject to this act and under what act it is organized.
(b) A statement that the purpose of becoming a member of a cooperative is to assure access to the goods, services, and facilities of the cooperative and not to gain profit.
(c) A statement of voting rights and rights to notice of meetings of members.
(d) A statement of the qualifications for admission to and retention of membership and the right of the cooperative to terminate membership, if any.
(e) A statement of the restrictions, if any, on the transfer of memberships.
(f) A statement of the rights to redemption of a member capital, if any, or a statement that member capital is not redeemable.
(g) A statement of the right of members to call special meetings or cause a mail ballot, to receive annual reports, and to secure other material information concerning the cooperative.

450.3139 Redemption of member capital; failure to patronize cooperative; notice of redemption; failure to respond and claim payment; failure to claim refunds of patronage capital, deposits, and fees; failure of nonmember patron to pay in or accumulate full member capital or comply with bylaws.

Sec. 1139.

(1) Unless the articles or bylaws provide that the member capital is not redeemable, upon termination of a membership issued on a member capital basis, a cooperative shall redeem the member's member capital by paying to the member in cash or other property (i) the lesser of the member's member capital or the member's pro rata share of the total member capital of the cooperative determined according to the ratio each member's member capital bears to total member capital, unless a different proration is provided in the articles; or (ii) such other amount as may be provided in the articles or bylaws. Payment shall be made within 5 years from the date of termination, unless the articles or bylaws provide for a different period for payment.

(2) Unless the articles or bylaws provide that member capital is not redeemable, a cooperative may adopt and implement any plan to partially redeem member capital.

(3) A cooperative shall not redeem member capital or any portion thereof under either of the following conditions:
   (a) When the cooperative is insolvent or when the redemption would render the cooperative insolvent.
   (b) Unless after redemption there remains outstanding 1 or more classes of members possessing among them, collectively, voting rights.

(4) The articles or bylaws may provide that if a member fails to patronize a cooperative to an extent and within a specific period of time, the membership shall be terminated.

(5) A person entitled to payment for redemption of member capital shall be given reasonable notice of the redemption, which notice may be by mail to the last known address of the person. If the person fails to respond to the notice and claim the payment within 5 years from the date of notice, that person shall have no further rights in the member capital and the member capital may be added to the general funds of the cooperative.

(6) In the case of a nonprofit power corporation as described in section 261(4), any refunds of patronage capital, deposits, and fees of members

not claimed within 5 years after reasonable notice has been given to the member's last known address shall remain the property of the corporation. If any such refund is not claimed by the member within the 5-year period, the member shall have no claim to the refund.

(7) The articles or bylaws may provide that if within any time specified in the bylaws or articles any nonmember patron who has subscribed for membership has not paid in or accumulated the full member capital required for membership or has failed to comply with the provisions of the bylaws, if any, concerning admission to membership, any amounts allocated from net savings and credited to the member capital of the nonmember patron may be added to the general funds of the cooperative and thereafter the nonmember patron shall have no further rights therein.

450.3141 Meetings; petitions; signatures; quorum.

Sec. 1141.

Regular meetings of members shall be held at a time and place prescribed in the bylaws but not less than annually. A special meeting of members may be called by the board of directors or by written petition of members. A petition shall state the purpose or purposes for which the meeting is to be called. Unless the bylaws provide for a smaller percent or number, the number of member signatures required for such a petition shall be 10% of the members. Notwithstanding section 415, unless the articles or bylaws provide a greater percentage or number, a quorum shall be 10% of the members or 50 members, whichever is less.

450.3143 Alternative notice of regular meeting.

Sec. 1143.

Instead of the notice required in section 404, written notice of the time, place, and purposes of a regular meeting of members may be given by a means specified in the bylaws and accessible to all members, if the date of regular meeting is established in the bylaws and the notice is made accessible to all members at least 15 days before the meeting.

450.3144 Proxies; voting by mail ballot, referendum, or electronic transmission.

Sec. 1144.

(1) Notwithstanding section 421, there shall be no proxies unless the articles of incorporation or bylaws authorize use of proxies. If the articles of incorporation or bylaws authorize use of proxies, an individual may not vote more than 5 proxies at any meeting.
(2) The articles or bylaws may provide a method by which members may vote on matters submitted to a vote of members by mail ballot, referendum, or electronic transmission.

450.3145 Amendments; affirmative vote of majority.

Sec. 1145.

Notwithstanding section 611(4), 703(2), 753(4), or 804(4), unless the articles of incorporation provide for a higher vote for passage, amendment of the articles of incorporation, amendment of the bylaws which alters member voting rights or member capital, merger, consolidation, disposition of all or substantially all of the assets of the corporation, or dissolution shall be adopted by the affirmative vote of a majority of the votes cast by members eligible to vote thereon, and if a class is eligible to vote thereon as a class, the affirmative vote of a majority of the votes cast by members of each class. Such action may only be taken at a meeting called according to the notice provisions of section 404.

450.3146 Effective date of adopted action; confirmation vote; filing with administrator.

Sec. 1146.

(1) An action subject to the vote requirement of section 1145 shall not take effect for 60 days from the date of adoption and shall be subject to 1 confirmation vote as provided in subsection (2) if the action is adopted by less than a majority of all the members eligible to vote.
(2) If a petition of 15% or more of the members eligible to vote is presented to the cooperative prior to the sixtieth day after the adoption of the action, the cooperative shall cause a confirmation vote to be held. The cooperative shall cause a special meeting or, if authorized, mail ballot or referendum to be conducted within 45 days of receipt of the petition. The confirmation vote must achieve the vote which would have been required

for original adoption. If confirmed, the action or amendment may take effect immediately after the confirmation or upon filing with the administrator, if such filing is required.

(3) If an action or amendment is subject to confirmation, a filing shall not be made with the administrator until the time for presenting a petition has expired or the action is confirmed.

450.3147 Dispute resolution body.

Sec. 1147.

A cooperative may authorize in its articles or bylaws the establishment of a neutral dispute resolution body. The dispute resolution body shall attempt to settle disputes between the cooperative and any of its members. It shall be composed of individuals who are approved by both parties to the dispute, which individuals may be members or nonmembers, but not officers or directors of the cooperative. The bylaws of a cooperative may provide that membership in the cooperative is conditioned upon participation in good faith in the dispute resolution process authorized by this section.

450.3148 Purchase or sale under execution, in course of bankruptcy, or by legal process or operation of law; pledge of certificate; assignment of proprietary lease or other agreement.

Sec. 1148.

(1) The purchase or sale of any member capital or privileges in a cooperative made under execution, or in the course of bankruptcy proceedings, or by any legal process or by operation of law, shall not give any person any membership right, title, or interest in a cooperative, unless in accordance with the articles or bylaws of the cooperative.

(2) No subsequent amendment to the articles or bylaws shall invalidate or otherwise impair a pledge of a certificate issued under section 1136 or an assignment of a proprietary lease or other agreement providing for occupancy of facilities furnished by the cooperative, if the pledge or assignment was made when the articles or bylaws expressly permitted the pledge or assignment in connection with loans made to members.

450.3149 Books for recording operations; annual report, balance sheet, and income statement; certified report of condition; copies of reports;

mailings at request and expense of member; notice of member's desire to be contacted by other members regarding proposal.

Sec. 1149.

(1) A cooperative shall keep a set of books for recording its operations. A written report, including a statement of the amount of its transactions with members and the amount of its transactions with nonmember patrons, a balance sheet, and an income statement shall be prepared annually.

(2) A cooperative shall prepare, not later than 120 days after the close of its fiscal year, a report of its condition, which report shall be certified by the president. The report shall include all of the following:
    (a) The name and principal address of the cooperative.
    (b) The names, addresses, and date of expiration of terms of the officers and directors, and their rate of compensation, if any.
    (c) The number of memberships granted and terminated and the amount of member capital paid in during the fiscal year.

(3) A copy of the reports required by this section shall be presented at the annual membership meeting or distributed to each member. Copies of the report shall be kept on file at the principal office of the cooperative and shall be made available to members, subscribers, and applicants for membership during regular business hours. In addition, copies of the report shall be mailed to a member upon written request by the member.

(4) If a membership address list is not accessible to members, then any mailing reasonably related to the affairs of the membership shall be made by a cooperative at the request and expense of a member.

(5) If a member makes a timely request in writing that a cooperative notify the membership of the member's desire to be contacted by other members regarding a proposal then pending for vote by the membership, the cooperative shall include in the next communication sent by the cooperative to all members, if any, a brief notice of that member's request which shall identify the member and shall state whether the member is for or against the proposal and how to contact that member.

450.3151 Initial board of directors; membership; term.

Sec. 1151.

Notwithstanding section 505, the initial board of directors of a cooperative shall consist of at least 5 persons. The term of office of directors shall be no more than 3 years.

450.3152 Board of directors; election or appointment other than by vote of membership.

Sec. 1152.

Notwithstanding section 505, the bylaws of a cooperative may provide for 1/3 or less of the board of directors to be elected or appointed other than by a vote of the membership.

450.3153 Affiliation with another organization; section inapplicable to allocations of net savings.

Sec. 1153.

A vote of the membership shall be required to affiliate with another organization involving the investment of more than 30% of the assets of the cooperative, if the affiliation is not in the usual and regular course of its business. This section shall not apply to any allocations of net savings to the cooperative by any person.

450.3161 Amendment to articles of incorporation; calling special meeting; consideration of proposed amendment.

Sec. 1161.

An amendment to the articles of incorporation may be proposed by the board, by 10% or more of the members, or by some smaller percentage of members established in the articles or bylaws. If proposed by the number of members required for calling a special meeting pursuant to section 1141, a special meeting shall be called within a reasonable time. If proposed by less than the number of members required to call a special meeting, then the proposed amendment shall be considered at the next annual or special meeting.

450.3162 Distribution of assets generally.

Sec. 1162.

In the event of an amendment to the articles or bylaws, merger, consolidation, or disposition of substantially all of the assets of the cooperative, or dissolution, which results in a distribution of all or substantially all of the assets of the corporation to members, the distribution shall be in the manner and order provided in section 1183.

450.3183 Distribution of assets upon dissolution; distribution of assets held for charitable or similar purpose; redemption of investment certificates.

Sec. 1183.

(1) Notwithstanding section 855, upon dissolution, the assets of a cooperative shall be distributed in the following manner and order:
  (a) By paying or providing for payment of its debts and expenses.
  (b) By redeeming member capital by paying to the member in cash or other property (i) the lesser of the member's member capital or the member's pro rata share of total member capital of the cooperative determined according to the ratio each member's member capital bears to total member capital, unless a different proration is provided in the articles; or (ii) such other amount as may be provided in the articles or bylaws.
  (c) By distributing any surplus to (i) those patrons who have been members or subscribers at any time during not less than the 6 years preceding dissolution or since formation of the cooperative, whichever is less, on the basis of patronage during that period; (ii) any other cooperative, foreign cooperative, or nonprofit organization designated by membership resolution; or (iii) both.
(2) Assets held by a cooperative for a charitable or similar purpose shall be distributed pursuant to section 855(c).
(3) Investment certificates issued pursuant to section 1137 shall be redeemed according to the terms of the certificates.

450.3191 Foreign cooperative.

Sec. 1191.

A foreign cooperative shall be entitled to conduct its affairs in this state upon complying with the provisions of chapter 10 and, if a consumer cooperative, by agreeing to provide its members and patrons residing in this state reasonable notice of their membership rights. Reasonable notice shall be considered given if written notice of the matters required to be disclosed by section 1132 is provided to each patron residing in this state and written notice of the matters required to be disclosed by section 1138 is provided to each member residing in this state.

450.3192 Election by corporation to accept act and chapter; procedure; effect of filing certificate of election.

Sec. 1192.

(1) Any corporation may elect to accept this act and this chapter as follows:
 (a) The board of directors shall adopt a resolution recommending that the corporation accept this act and this chapter and directing that the question of acceptance be submitted to a vote at a meeting of the members or stockholders entitled to vote thereon. Written notice stating that the purpose, or 1 of the purposes, of the meeting is to consider electing to accept this act and this chapter, shall be given to each member and stockholder entitled to vote at the meeting, within the time and in the manner provided in this act for the giving of notice of meetings of members. The election to accept this act and this chapter shall require for adoption that vote which is required by that corporation to amend its articles of incorporation.
 (b) A certificate of election to accept the act and this chapter shall be filed in accordance with section 131. The certificate shall set forth:
  (i) The name of the corporation.
  (ii) A statement by the corporation that it has elected to accept this act and this chapter.
  (iii) A statement setting forth the date of the meeting of members or stockholders at which the election to accept this act and this chapter was made, that a quorum was present at the meeting, and that the acceptance was authorized by that vote which is required by the corporation to amend its articles of incorporation.
  (iv) If the corporation has issued shares of stock, a statement of that fact including the number of shares issued and outstanding, and a statement that all issued and outstanding shares of stock will be canceled upon the filing of the

statement and that from and after the effective date of filing the authority of the corporation to issue shares of stock shall be terminated.
   (v) A statement of the manner and basis of converting shares or memberships, voting rights, and equity interests into memberships, voting rights, and member capital subject to this chapter.
(2) Upon filing of the certificate of election, the election of the corporation to accept this act and this chapter shall become effective and the corporation shall have the same powers and privileges and be subject to the same duties, restrictions, penalties, and liabilities as though the corporation had been originally organized under this act and this chapter.

www.ingramcontent.com/pod-product-compliance
Lightning Source LLC
Chambersburg PA
CBHW051706170526
45167CB00002B/550